P-40 Warhawk Aces of the MTO

SERIES EDITOR: TONY HOLMES

OSPREY AIRCRAFT OF THE ACES® • 43

P-40 Warhawk Aces of the MTO

Carl Molesworth

OSPREY
PUBLISHING

Front cover
The single most successful mission ever flown by P-40 Warhawk pilots of the USAAF took place on 18 April 1943, and the action became known as the 'Palm Sunday Massacre'. Acting on an intelligence report that the *Afrika Korps* was planning a massive evacuation flight from Cape Bon, Tunisia, to Sicily, the 57th FG launched a patrol of 48 P-40s of the 64th, 65th, 66th and 314th FSs from El Djem at 1705 hrs. With RAF Spitfire IXs of No 92 Sqn flying top cover, the formation intercepted a huge V-formation of Luftwaffe Ju 52/3m tri-motor transports, escorted by Bf 109s, flying low over the Bay of Tunis in a north-easterly direction. The P-40s attacked, and in the melee that followed Capt Roy E 'Deke' Whittaker of the 65th FS scored four of the USAAF's 76 confirmed kills, boosting his victory tally to seven, and making him the highest-scoring ace in the legendary 57th FG. Whittaker, who was flying group CO Col Art Salisbury's P-40F 'White 01' at the time, gave the following account of the battle;

'I attacked the Ju 52s from astern at high speed and fired at two planes in the leading formation. The bursts were short, and the only effect I saw was pieces flying off the cabin of the second ship. I pulled away and circled to the right, and then made my second attack. I fired two bursts into two more '52s – again in the leading formation. They both burst into flames. The second flew a little distance and then crashed into the water. I lost sight of the first and didn't see it hit. I then made a third pass and sent a good burst into the left of the formation, at another Junkers. As I pulled away, it crashed into the water. By that time the Me-109s were among us. As I pulled up to the left, I saw a '109 dive through an element of four Warhawks, and I tagged on his underside and gave him a long burst in the belly. He crashed into the sea from a thousand feet. I then joined up with some Warhawks that were "lufberrying" with six Me-109s. I met one of these fighters with a quartering attack and hit him with a short burst. Pieces flew from the plane and he started smoking, but he climbed out of the fight'
(*cover artwork by Iain Wyllie*)

First published in Great Britain in 2002 by Osprey Publishing, Elms Court, Chapel Way, Botley, Oxford, OX2 9LP

ISBN 1 84176 288 1

Edited by Tony Holmes
Page design by Tony Truscott
Cover Artwork by Iain Wyllie
Aircraft Profiles by Jim Laurier
Scale Drawings by Mark Styling
Origination by Grasmere Digital Imaging, Leeds, UK
Printed through Bookbuilders, Hong Kong

02 03 04 05 06   10 9 8 7 6 5 4 3 2 1

ACKNOWLEDGEMENTS:
This author offers sincere thanks to the many veterans of service in the MTO, and their families, who provided me with the photographs, documents and personal recollections that made this book possible.

I offer special thanks to Dwayne Tabatt, who provided nearly all of the photo coverage of the 325th FG, and George E Dively Jr, 33rd FG historian. Others who contributed include Elizabeth and Ken Adams, Paul Andricson, Dana Bell, Steve Blake, Muriel Brewer, Craig Busby, Thomas Chase, James V Crow, Dave Fenex, Tom Ivie, Howard Levy, Marilyn Maloney, William Marshall, El Geva McCleary, Babs Mease, Griff Murphey, Suzi Riddle, Martin Ruegsegger, Melinda Shobe, Sabra Fenex Smith, Barry Thomas, Roy Whittaker Jr and Gil Wymond III. I would also like to recognise the work of researchers and authors Thomas M Boyle, Norman Brandman, John M Campbell, Joe Christy, Bill Colgan, Benjamin O Davis Jr, Lou Drendel, Jeff Ethell, Charles E Francis, John Guenther, William N Hess, Edward Jablonski, Frederick A Johnsen, Bert Kinzey, Gerd Lanio, John Louks, Ernest R McDowell, Frank Olynyk, James E Reed, Kenn C Rust, Albert Schoenfeld, Jerry Scutts, Christopher Shores, Louis L Snyder, Mike Spick, John Stanaway, Jim Sullivan and Don Woerpel. Finally, the Air Force Historical Research Agency and Maxwell Air Force Base provided invaluable historical records compiled by many of the units involved.

Back cover photograph
A helmeted groundcrewman poses next to a P-40F displaying three swastika victory markings beneath its windscreen at Thelepte in early 1943. This machine may have been assigned to Maj Mark Hubbard, 59th FS CO, who scored his third victory on 1 February 1943 – his score stood at four kills by the time he finished his tour in the MTO in late 1943. Hubbard would go on to achieve ace status on 18 March 1944 while serving as CO of the P-38J-equipped 20th FG in England. He had little chance to celebrate 'acedom', however, for he was shot down on the same mission that he took his score past five kills! Hubbard spent the rest of the war as a PoW (*John Croder*)

CONTENTS

INTRODUCTION

P-40 Warhawk pilots of the United States Army Air Force assigned to the Mediterranean Theater of Operations (MTO) during World War 2 never achieved the notoriety accorded to their brothers-in-arms in the Pacific and in China. This is unfortunate, but perhaps not surprising.

Although P-40 squadrons played a key role in the air war over North Africa, Sicily and Italy during 1942-43, the press paid little attention to them. For the most part, they operated far from the media centres on desolate landing strips close to the frontlines. Their aeroplanes weren't sleek new Lightnings nor legendary Spitfires, but the ubiquitous Curtiss P-40, a type better known at the time for its performance shortcomings than for its attributes of outstanding toughness and versatility. Maybe even more important in the eyes of the contemporary press, P-40 pilots in the MTO did not run up big personal scores of enemy aircraft destroyed.

But shooting down enemy aircraft was not the primary task of these Warhawk pilots. They were engaged in fighter-bomber operations, the forerunner of what is known today as tactical aviation. Their job was to batter enemy ground forces from their frontline positions to their lines of communications and supply, many miles to the rear. Some days their assignments were direct bombing and strafing attacks, and on other occasions they would provide fighter escort for medium bombers. If enemy aircraft attempted to intervene, the P-40 pilots were expected to fight them off and then complete their primary bombing mission. It was a rare day indeed when P-40s were sent out with the express purpose of seeking and destroying Axis aircraft, but they could do that, too, with vicious effectiveness. Just ask any Messerschmitt pilot who encountered them over Marble Arch, Cape Bon, Sardinia or Anzio.

Despite its shortcomings, the Curtiss P-40 was an excellent weapon for this type of air combat. It was never the fastest nor highest climbing aeroplane in the sky, but it was tough, reliable, well armed, and capable of carrying a substantial bomb load over a respectable range. And unlike in China and the Pacific, it was more manoeuvrable than were the enemy fighters it encountered. P-40 pilots in the MTO may have wished they were flying more modern Lightnings, Thunderbolts or Mustangs, but the Warhawk was the only American fighter available to them at the time, so they made the best of it.

It is a little recognised fact that the P-40 was the most numerous American fighter in the MTO until early 1944, equipping five full fighter groups at its peak during the summer of 1943. The pilots in these units were credited with a respectable total of 592 confirmed victories in P-40s, and 16 of them reached 'ace' status with five or more enemy aircraft destroyed. This is their story.

I have always had a soft spot for stories about underdogs, so I took on the challenge of writing about Warhawk pilots in the MTO with great enthusiasm. My only regret is that the limitations of this book did not allow me to also detail the outstanding service rendered by the ground personnel who supported the pilots. They suffered through the sand storms, the floods, the flies, the bad food, the bombing and strafing raids, the artillery barrages, and the other miseries of life in the MTO, just as the pilots did. These men worked long hours in terrible conditions, and many of them did it for three years or longer before they went home. They are truly the unsung heroes of this story.

In the course of gathering material for this book, I have made contact with many wonderful people who have connections to the P-40 units of the MTO. As I write this, I am looking at two storage bins full to bursting with personal accounts, photographs, official documents, books and other items that they sent me related to their experiences, or the experiences of loved ones. I sincerely appreciate the trust they have placed in me to tell this story, and I only wish I could have incorporated something from each of them into this book.

Carl Molesworth
Washington
September 2001

WARHAWKS OVER 'THE BLUE'

The teletype in the headquarters office of the 57th Fighter Group (FG) at East Boston, Massachusetts, began to clatter on the morning of 24 June 1942 with a message from the Eastern Defense Command Headquarters, United States Army Air Force. This was not unusual. For six months, since the Japanese attack on Pearl Harbor plunged the US into World War 2, the 57th FG had been receiving a steady stream of orders and instructions as it worked up to combat readiness while providing air defence for the New England area of the USA.

On this day, however, the teletype spat out a message that everyone in the unit had been anticipating for months. In the terse language of the military, Special Order No 168 told 72 pilots that they were going into combat.

'The officers on the attached roster . . . will proceed without delay to Mitchell Field, New York, reporting to the commanding general, I Fighter Command', the order stated. 'Upon completion of this temporary duty they will proceed to station outside limits of Continental United States. This is a permanent change of station. Dependants will not accompany any of these officers'.

The 57th FG had been activated on 15 January 1941. The war in Europe was already in its 17th month by then, and American leaders could see the likelihood of their own nation being drawn into the conflict. US military forces had been badly neglected during the Great Depression of the 1930s, and now a mad dash was beginning to bring it back up to strength.

Growth came in fits and starts for the 57th FG during 1941, as men were assigned to the unit out of training schools and just as rapidly transferred back out, after gaining a little experience, to form the nuclei of other new combat units being formed. Likewise, the number of Curtiss P-40 fighters assigned to the group grew slowly over the course of the year

When the United States entered World War 2 in December 1941, the 57th FG was initially assigned to provide air defence in the New England area. Here, a 64th FS P-40C is prepared for a flight at Bradley Field, Connecticut. It bears the tail code '22/57P' (barely legible) in yellow on its fin (*Lou Lederman*)

— see *Osprey Aircraft of the Aces 35 - P-40 Warhawk Aces of the CBI*, for more information about the development of the Curtiss P-40.

By October 1941, the group was considered of sufficient strength and experience to conduct a cross-country exercise. Leaving from its main base in Windsor Locks, Connecticut, the 57th FG flew all the way across the nation to McChord Field, Washington. Bad weather and other problems plagued the flight, and the group lost nearly half of its 25 aeroplanes, with four pilots being killed in crashes.

Once back in New England, the 57th FG settled into a steady schedule of air defence patrols and practice missions, as its pilots and technicians honed their skills in preparation for deployment to a combat zone. With the arrival of Special Order 168, the men of the 57th knew they were on their way overseas. Topping the list of pilots was Maj Frank H Mears, who would serve as group commander. He and 27 other pilots were already members of the 57th FG – the rest were drawn from two other fighter groups, the 33rd and 56th, then still in training. Now the big question for the pilots was where were they going?

The answer, or at least a pretty strong hint, awaited them at Mitchell Field, where the USAAF had assembled 72 brand-new Curtiss P-40F Warhawks for the 57th FG to take overseas. These aeroplanes differed from the P-40s that the pilots had been flying in two key ways. Most importantly, the F-model was powered by the Packard V-1650-1 Merlin engine, a license-built version of the superlative Rolls-Royce powerplant installed in British Spitfires and Hurricanes. This engine was similar in size and output to the Allison V-1710 installed in earlier (and later) versions of the P-40, but its superior supercharging system allowed it to produce full power at higher altitudes than the Allison could reach.

The strongest clue, however, lay in the camouflage scheme that each of the P-40Fs had been adorned with. It was not the ubiquitous Olive Drab

Pilots of the 65th FS/57th FG pose in their flying gear in front of the sandbagged operations building at Groton, Connecticut, shortly after the declaration of war. The squadron commander, Capt Philip G Cochran, is standing third from the right. The others are, from left to right, 2Lt Gilbert O Wymond, unknown, 1Lt Arthur G Salisbury, 2Lt Thomas W Clark, 2Lt Roy Whittaker and unknown. Both Salisbury and Wymond would later command the squadron, and the former also commanded the 57th FG from December 1942 through to April 1944 (*Ed Silks*)

that the pilots were accustomed to seeing. These Warhawks had been finished in a colour the Army called 'Desert Tan', although the paint exhibited a distinctly pinkish hue. Where else could the 57th be going with aircraft painted this way but to the deserts of North Africa?

June 1942 was a critical month for the British Commonwealth forces fighting in North Africa. Their see-saw war had started two years earlier, when Italy declared war on Great Britain in June 1940. The RAF in Egypt immediately launched air attacks against the Italians in neighbouring Libya. Emboldened by their German ally's successes in northern Europe, the Italians then advanced eastward into Egypt in September 1940.

A British counterattack in December pushed them back, and within two months, British forces had advanced some 1000 miles to El Agheila, capturing more than 100,000 Italian troops in the process. To head off further disaster, Germany entered the desert war at this point.

German General Erwin Rommel and his soon-to-be-famous *Afrika Korps* attacked in April 1941, and within two weeks the British had been pushed all the way back into Egypt. There, a stalemate developed, as German resources were diverted to the Nazi attack on the Soviet Union. The British mounted a second campaign late in the year, and by mid-January 1942 they again were deep inside Libya. But once more, their success was fleeting, for Rommel struck back on 26 May 1942 at Gazala and pushed British forces all the way back to El Alamein, in Egypt, which was less than 100 miles from Alexandria.

Just as Rommel's advance was picking up steam, British Prime Minister Winston Churchill arrived in Washington, DC, to discuss war plans with US president Franklin D Roosevelt. Early on, the two leaders had agreed on a 'Europe first' policy for the defeat of the Axis powers. American-made war materials were being shipped across the Atlantic at a ferocious pace, but thus far Roosevelt had been reluctant to commit US combat forces to the European conflict piecemeal. He preferred to build up American forces to sufficient strength to open a second front on the continent with one smashing blow.

Now, however, with the British backed up in Egypt again and Soviet leader Josef Stalin demanding relief from the German invasion of his country as well, Roosevelt agreed to commit American combat units to North Africa. Among them would be six fighter groups of the USAAF, the first of which was to be operational in-theatre by 1 September 1942. That group would be the 57th FG.

Pilots began arriving at Mitchell Field within 25 hours of receiving Special Order No 168. There, they were surprised to learn that they would be travelling overseas on a US Navy aircraft carrier, and that they would have to fly their P-40s off the ship when they arrived at their destination.

One of those pilots was 2Lt Dale Deniston, who had transferred in from the 33rd FG. He described his short stay at Mitchell in his privately published book, *Memories of a Fighter Pilot*;

'I went up to Mitchell Field on the early morning train. When we arrived at the base, the airfield contained 75 brand new P-40Fs painted a pink colour, which we guessed might be desert camouflage. We were processed with shots, dental and physical exams, and drew sidearms, winter flying gear and all sorts of stuff. Then we met our aeroplanes –

mine was number "84". All the aircraft were brand new, with only four hours total engine and flight time on each of them.

'We flew the aircraft on a number of occasions prior to embarking, and several Navy pilots were on hand to instruct us in carrier take-offs. They painted lines on the runway to indicate about 1000 ft. We were to set flaps, set trim tabs to compensate for torque, run the engine up to full power, hold the stick back, and then release brakes. Into the wind, I think the least distance we were able to get airborne was 1200 ft.

'We flew several squadron flights from Mitchell, and on the final one we didn't come back. Instead, we were directed to Quonset Point, Rhode Island, Naval Air Station. As I circled for landing at Quonset Point, I spotted an aircraft carrier in port. After landing, sailors along the runway directed me to taxy off the runway and down a road right to the dock. I taxied up to the dock next to the carrier and was given the sign to cut the engine. As I sat in the cockpit filling out my Form I report, sailors were climbing all over my aircraft and removing my engine cowling.

'A sailor said, "Lieutenant, you will have to get out now, we are taking it aboard". The hoist came down, was attached to the engine mount, and my bird was taken up to the flightdeck of the USS *Ranger*. Soon all the aircraft and pilots (including six alternate pilots in case of illness) were aboard, and we were at sea – destination unknown.'

The 57th's carrier deployment was not unprecedented – the *Ranger* had delivered a shipment of 68 P-40E-1s to Accra, on the Gold Coast of Africa, in late May 1942. These aircraft were then ferried across Africa and the Middle East to India, where they served as replacements in the 51st FG. Some of them even went on to see combat in China. The 57th FG would not be going quite so far, as the pilots learned shortly after the *Ranger* put to sea.

But the 57th would be the first USAAF group to deploy via carrier as a unit. Its pilots, too, would fly off the *Ranger* to Accra, but their destination was Egypt, where they would serve as part of the RAF's Desert Air Force (DAF). First, however, was the small matter of taking off from a Navy carrier in an Army fighter not known for its climbing performance.

On 19 July 1942, the *Ranger* turned into the wind about 100 miles off the African coast, and newly-promoted Lt Col Mears gunned his P-40F 'White 01' *Regina IV* down the deck to lead the first of four 18-ship flights to Accra. Nearly three hours later, Capt Archie Knight of group headquarters flew off in the last aeroplane. 2Lt Bill Mount of the 64th FS recalled his take-off;

'We had tried practice take-offs at Mitchell Field and had gotten off in between 1150 and 1300 ft into a 20-knot wind. The Navy told us the deck was 750 ft long, and heading into the wind made a big difference. It was only after we were aboard that we learned that the rear half of the deck would be full of P-40s, and that we were only to use the front half – 350 ft. That's when we got a little worried.

'I took off between the 30th and 40th aircraft. Only one pilot made a dip off the end of the flight deck – Roy Whittaker – and since he was a pretty good showman, we thought he did it on purpose.

'We had been required to run all our trim tab controls to both extreme positions every day during the voyage in order to avoid corrosion. As a result, when I went up to take off, I had forgotten to reset the tabs. The

One of the original pilots in the 65th FS/57th FG was 2Lt Roy E 'Deke' Whittaker, shown here with one of his squadron's P-40Es in early 1942. Whittaker would go on to score seven victories in North Africa, making him the top ace of the 57th FG (*Ed Silks*)

aeroplane was trimmed full tail heavy and full left rudder. I spent the takeoff roll trying to adjust tabs and fighting the controls. We had also covered the canopies with some stuff to eliminate sun reflections. In the damp climate off the Nigerian coast, the condensation had mixed with the "goop" so it was impossible to see out with the canopy closed, so I left it open. I probably started becoming deaf at that point.

'Landing at Accra was no problem – the runway was long and wide. We did damage a few with ground loops, however (not me). We had loaded a few rounds of ammunition because some of the territory we were to fly over was Vichy French – not friendly. The rest of the ammunition boxes were filled with cigarettes.'

The P-40s only stayed at Accra long enough to refuel. Then, with RAF bombers leading, they pressed on eastward in smaller flights, reaching Lagos, in Nigeria, by evening. Over the next week-and-a-half they made their way across the continent in hops of 100 to 300 miles. By the first of August, they had reached Muqueibila, in Palestine, where the group would spend several weeks learning how to fight in the desert, RAF-style.

Meanwhile, the ground personnel of the 57th FG had been split into two groups. A small advance echelon of 42 technicians was flown directly from the US to Palestine, arriving on 14 July 1942 to prepare for the arrival of the group's aircraft. The rest travelled by ship across the Atlantic, around Africa, and up the Red Sea, arriving in Palestine on 19 August. Meanwhile, the USAAF's fledgling Ninth Air Force, which would command American air power in the desert, was getting organised in Cairo as a subordinate unit of the DAF.

With combat-experienced RAF pilots serving as instructors, the pilots of the 57th began a series of practice missions. The RAF men were impressed with the flying skills of their new American allies, many of whom had hundreds of hours of P-40 time, and immediately began training them in their new role – fighter-bombing.

Over the past two years, the DAF had developed tactics that expanded the capabilities of its fighter force by employing it primarily against Axis ground targets in the desert. The fighters served as long-range artillery, sweeping behind Axis lines targeting communication and supply routes, as well as attacking enemy ground forces directly on the battlefield. If Axis aircraft were encountered, the fighters could jettison their bombs and protect themselves.

Typically, the DAF formation performing a fighter-bomber mission would divide itself, using half its strength as an assault flight and the other half as top-cover escort. Of course, the fighters were also used for more traditional tasks, such as fighter sweeps, interceptions and bomber escorts.

The P-40 was particularly well suited for this role. Never the best performing fighter in the sky, it was nevertheless reliable, carried heavy armament and could withstand

64th FS/57th FG armourer Sgt Rade Chuich cleans the guns of a Warhawk in the desert. The white spot on the aeroplane's lower cowling will soon be decorated with the squadron's 'Black Scorpion' badge. Note also how the P-40's original dark camouflage is wearing through the top coat of desert tan (*Lyle Custer*)

Armourers from the 66th FS/57th FG use a home-made lifting rack to ease the mounting of a 500-lb bomb under the belly of a P-40K Warhawk. The three small protrusions under the wing at right are attachment points for smaller 40-lb weapons (*Lou Lederman*)

The squadrons of the 57th FG had to move frequently to keep up with the advancing 8th Army after the stalemate at El Alamein was broken in early November 1942. Here, the trucks of the 66th FS prepare to head west, bound for a new landing ground (*Frank Hertzberg*)

amazing amounts of battle damage and still bring its pilot home safely. The Merlin-powered P-40Fs of the 57th FG were fitted with six 0.50-calibre machine guns, and they also boasted attachment points under the wings and fuselage centreline that allowed them to carry an assortment of light and heavy bombs.

And although the aeroplane's climb performance was sluggish and its combat effectiveness limited to low and medium altitudes up to 20,000 ft, it was more manoeuvrable than the German Bf 109 and Italian C.202 fighters it would face, and it was also a spectacular diver.

The RAF informed the 'green' pilots of the 57th FG that air-to-air combat tactics in the desert were not much removed from those used over the Western Front during World War 1 – keep your head on a swivel, and always 'beware of the Hun in the sun'.

Attacks were likely to come from above, with Axis pilots converting the superior altitude capabilities of their aircraft into speed in a diving attack. The best defence, RAF Kittyhawk pilots had learned, was to turn into the attack and bring the P-40's heavy firepower to bear in a head-on pass.

FIRST IN 'THE BLUE'

While training proceeded in Palestine, small groups of 57th FG pilots began moving up to the frontline in Egypt to gain actual combat experience with the DAF. These pilots (initially unit commanders and flight leaders) were assigned to Kittyhawk and Tomahawk squadrons. They would fly as wingmen to combat veterans during their first fighter-bomber sorties over the western desert – or in DAF parlance, 'The Blue'. Here, in the barren lands west of the Nile River, they would fight for nearly a year.

It was on these makeshift landing grounds just east of El Alamein, and about 100 miles west of the Egyptian port city of Alexandria, that the pilots got their first taste of desert life. It was not, perhaps, what they expected. Rather than the flowing sand dunes they had seen in the old silent movies of Rudolph Valentino, the land here on the coastal plain was featureless and hard.

A landing ground was merely a flat spot cleared of rocks, with four 55-gallon drums defining the boundaries of the runway, a wind sock in the middle and a village of tents off to one side, where the men lived and worked. There were no permanent buildings and no revetments. The only paved surface was the narrow coastal highway that

Groundcrews toiled under brutal conditions in North Africa. Here, a bronzed mechanic dressed only in shorts, shoes and a cap works on a P-40F that is undergoing an open-air engine change (*Dale Deniston*)

S/Sgt Lou Lederman, a crew chief in the 66th FS/57th FG, mans the anti-aircraft gun he rigged by mounting a German Spandau machine gun from a downed Stuka on an upturned bicycle fork, attached to a tripod! (*Lou Lederman*)

ran nearby. Water was as scarce as flies were plentiful. In fact, one veteran of this period told the author that the best way to spot someone who had been in the desert for a long time was to watch him eat. If the man could get a piece of food into his mouth without swallowing a fly, he had been in 'The Blue' long enough to develop the skill.

The crude conditions would harden the Americans rapidly. Although not as unruly as the civilian pilots who flew in China in Claire Chennault's American Volunteer Group, 57th FG personnel became similarly irregular in regard to uniforms and military bearing. If anything, they were more unkempt than the AVG pilots because the shortage of water made bathing and washing clothes a luxury. There was also an element of danger just being on a desert landing ground, because there was nowhere to hide during frequent enemy air attacks. Slit trenches hacked out of the rocky soil offered scant protection from bullets and bomb fragments.

On top of all that was the weather. No one was surprised to find the desert blazing hot and dry, but they soon learned it could also become cold and damp. Adding to that were the frequent dust storms, when huge clouds of wind-blown sand would blow up from the south and shut down everything for days at a time. With visibility at zero and stinging sand flying everywhere, there was nothing the men could do during these storms but sit in their tents and wait them out.

The 57th FG's first orientation missions took place on 9 August 1942. The P-40 pilots' first

1Lt John J Stefanik of the 66th FS/57th FG examines combat damage that he picked up in P-40F 'White 72' during a scrap with Bf 109s. The tough Warhawk lost its radio, but it brought Stefanik home unhurt (*via Dan and Melinda Shobe*)

encounter with enemy aircraft came five days later. On the morning of 14 August 1942, six pilots of the 57th FG were assigned to fly with No 260 Sqn of the RAF while providing top cover for 12 South African Boston bombers attacking Fuka Station. As the formation crossed the frontline near El Alamein, 14 Bf 109s attacked from out of the sun, and a whirling dogfight ensued.

1Lt William W O'Neill Jr of the 65th FS, flying on the wing of Australian ace Sgt Ron Cundy, spotted a Bf 109 below him to the right and broke off to attack it. He soon found himself overwhelmed by five Messerschmitt fighters, and after a brief, but fierce, fight was shot down and bailed out over the Mediterranean Sea. O'Neill landed close to shore, and was able to inflate his dinghy and paddle to the beach in Allied-held territory. On returning to his unit, O'Neill reported that he had shot down two Bf 109s, but his claims were never officially recognised.

The first accepted USAAF claim in the MTO came on 4 September 1942, when 2Lt Thomas T Williams of the 66th FS was credited with one Bf 109 probably destroyed. Williams was flying top cover with No 260 Sqn on a morning escort mission near El Alamein when the formation was attacked by several Bf 109s and C.202s. The enemy fighters came in from the north and made a run at the middle cover flight, leaving

2Lt Thomas T Williams of the 66th FS/57th FG was flying this P-40F-1 (41-13970) on 4 September 1942 when he scored the USAAF's first official air-to-air claim in the MTO – a Bf 109 probably destroyed. Shown here in about December 1942, after it had picked up the name *COUNT PISTOFF* and RAF fin flashes, 'White 95' was shot down on 11 January 1943, carrying its regular pilot, Lt W B 'Bill' Williams, to his death (*Dale Deniston*)

Six P-40s make a low pass over 2Lt Frank E Hertzberg's P-40F-1 'White 55' (41-13969). This 65th FS/57th FG Warhawk displays its serial in black on the rudder, and the aircraft number is repeated in red on the lower cowling. Later, Hertzberg named the aeroplane *Miss Harriet* for his future wife (*Frank Hertzberg*)

Blowing sand and dust played havoc with the working parts of aircraft in the desert. This 66th FS/57th FG Warhawk wears a canvas 'cocoon' for protection (*Lou Lederman*)

themselves vulnerable to the top cover P-40s. 2Lt Williams got a shot at one of the Bf 109s, and he saw his fire hitting home before he was forced to break off the engagement. A C.202 was also destroyed by an RAF pilot before the enemy aircraft fled the area.

By 13 September 1942 the pilots of the 57th FG had completed 158 sorties with their host RAF and South African Air Force (SAAF) squadrons. With training and orientation for desert flying now complete, the time had come to reunite the 57th FG so that it could begin operating as a unit. On 16 September, personnel from the group headquarters and the three squadrons – the 64th, 65th and 66th FSs – began converging on Landing Ground (LG) 174, which would be their new home.

The 57th FG was assigned to the RAF's No 211 Group, gaining full operational status on 7 October 1942. Two days later, the Americans recorded their first confirmed aerial victory. Six P-40Fs of the 64th FS, led by its commanding officer, Maj Clermont Wheeler, were escorting 18 Boston bombers attacking the enemy airfield at El Daba when the action occurred. One of the pilots flying with Maj Wheeler was 1Lt William J Mount, who recalled the mission more than 50 years later;

'I was lucky to get the first aerial victory in our unit. I was flying on Bob Barnum's wing, and our job was to provoke a response from the fighter unit at El Daba. We thought this would be unlikely, as there had been light rain the night before, which left the German field muddy. Barnum saw something and did a quick half roll and split-S that I could not follow.

'About that time I saw this lone Bf 109 fly across in front of me, heading out to sea. I was above him, and he was climbing. I tacked onto

his tail, dived slightly and caught up with him. I gave him a long burst and saw the aeroplane disintegrate, breaking in two behind the cockpit. It fell into the ocean. By then I was on my own and, as I recall, I returned straight to base.'

Mount would go on to fly 95 missions, claiming one further enemy aeroplane damaged, before completing his combat tour and returning to the US in May 1943.

Another 64th FS pilot taking part in the 9 October mission was 1Lt George D Mobbs, who had a much tougher time of it. He recorded this description in his diary;

'We got mixed up and got to the landing ground ahead of the bombers, but went in to strafe anyway. That is, most of us did. I was on the outside, and just as we started to go down, four or five '109s started to attack me. I turned into them and got a short burst at one, but it was a 90-degree deflection shot. Three of them kept attacking me, and I kept evading them, and occasionally getting a shot. Meanwhile, the rest of our aeroplanes had gone in to strafe and then flown out to sea, but I couldn't join them because the three German fighters kept on attacking me.

'I was running the engine at 55 to 65 inches of mercury and 3000 rpm, so I could pretty well stay with them. They would keep alternating the attacks between them. After a few minutes I got on one of their tails and was overtaking him. I didn't open fire until I was about 100 yards from him. I gave him a squirt and nothing happened. I moved over a little and changed my sighting, and on about the third burst his aeroplane burst into flames and fell off to one side. I was going to watch him go down so I would have a chance of getting credit for one destroyed, but one of the other jokers attacked so I was busy evading him. However, I spotted the first one moments later a few thousand feet below me, still spiralling down, but I never got another look at him after that.

'I was still in a hole. The other two kept attacking, one after the other. Later, I got a few shots at one from directly behind and slightly above as we were diving. I could see the aeroplane jerk each time I pulled the trigger but saw no debris or fire from it, and I was drawn away by the other one attacking. I must have hit the Jerry, because I never saw him again.

'Now I just had one to worry about, but on his next attack I finished my ammunition. He kept following and attacking, but with just him to worry about, I was making pretty good time back toward our lines. On another attack we met head-on, and I don't think he fired his guns. I didn't see them, anyway, and I was already out of ammunition.

'We were down pretty low by then – 1000 ft – and the German ack-ack had opened up at me. But I was going so fast that they were shooting behind me. I had everything forward. I was running awfully hard, and the ack-ack was getting pretty close to the Jerry pilot behind me. It was kind of amusing, because it looked as if I was going to make it back if my engine didn't quit. We were so low that I could see the ack-ack gun emplacements below.'

In fact, the engine in 1Lt Mobbs' P-40F did hold together, and the Bf 109 pilot gave up the chase. The American returned safely to base, where he was awarded one Bf 109 probably destroyed for the mission. Four days later, Mobbs recorded his first of four confirmed victories during a scrap with 20 Bf 109s over El Alamein. In this same engagement,

Lt Arnold D Jaqua recorded the first claims for the 65th FS – one Bf 109 destroyed and another damaged. Now all three squadrons within the 57th FG were 'on the board'.

———— FORWARD FROM EL ALAMEIN ————

Late in the evening of 23 October 1942, the heavy artillery of Lt Gen Bernard L Montgomery's British 8th Army opened fire against German positions along the 40-mile front at El Alamein. Troops had been massing on both sides of the front, which stretched southward from the beaches of the Mediterranean Sea to the impassable Qattara Depression, for seven weeks since the British had halted the most recent thrust by the *Afrika Korps*. Now the decisive battle of the two-year-old war in the desert was about to begin.

At first light on 24 October, some 230,000 men of the 8th Army began moving forward in three distinct thrusts against the 107,000 Italian and German troops facing them. Above the front, creating an umbrella over the Allied troops and a hailstorm of bombs and bullets for the enemy,

The P-40 pilot's most common and dangerous adversary in North Africa was the Luftwaffe's Messerschmitt Bf 109F/G fighter. 2./JG 27 left this unserviceable Bf 109F ('Red 11') behind when it hastily departed from Libya in November 1942 (*Andrew D'Antoni*)

The best Italian fighter encountered by American P-40 pilots in the MTO was the Macchi C.202, which was considered to be more manoeuvrable than the Bf 109. This example ('White 8') served with 356ª *Squadriglia* during the defence of Sicily in 1943 (*Clarence B Van Rossum Jr*)

were massed formations of DAF fighters and bombers.

No 211 Group boasted seven Kittyhawk squadrons and one Tomahawk squadron, plus three units each of Spitfires, Hurricanes and 57th FG Warhawks. A further eight Hurricane squadrons flew in No 212 Group, and nine bomber squadrons were equipped with Bostons, Baltimores and USAAF B-25 Mitchells. The primary Axis fighter forces opposing the Allied pilots were the three *gruppen* of the Luftwaffe's legendary JG 27, and one from JG 53, flying Bf 109F/Gs, plus seven Italian *Gruppi* equipped with Macchi C.202s.

Capt Lyman Middleditch Jr of the 64th FS/57th FG was the first ace of the Ninth Air Force. On 27 October 1942, during the advance from El Alamein, Middleditch shot down three Bf 109s in a single mission. He scored his fifth, and last, confirmed victory on 2 April 1943 (*Art Salisbury*)

The P-40F Warhawks of the 57th FG flew no fewer than three missions on 24 October, each time escorting Boston bombers, but had only one inconsequential encounter with enemy fighters during the day. A midday mission by the 64th FS on 25 October brought the initial victory for the pilot who would become the 57th FG's first ace, 1Lt Lyman Middleditch Jr, a 27-year-old New Yorker who had joined the squadron a few days before the USS *Ranger* deployment.

Middleditch was flying P-40F 'White 17' in a formation of eight P-40s assigned to attack LG 20 – a known Bf 109 base. On arrival over the target, mission leader Capt Glade 'Buck' Bilby noted dust rising from the airstrip, but no aircraft parked there. Obviously, enemy fighters had just taken off, so Bilby led his formation in a diving attack on a concentration of motor transports parked at the edge of the field. Shortly after the P-40s had released their bombs, five or more Bf 109s attacked them. The 64th FS mission report stated that, 'Lt Middleditch saw two Me-109s on Lt (Ernest D) Hartman's tail, made a right turn and gave the e/a a good burst. The e/a went into the sea'.

Lt Middleditch's victory was confirmed by three pilots who saw the Bf 109 go down. Two days later, Middleditch achieved one of the most spectacular successes in the early history of the 57th FG when he downing three Bf 109s in a single mission while flying in an eight-aeroplane 64th FS formation providing top cover for eight 65th FS fighter-bombers.

Shortly after the P-40s delivered their bombs on LG 20, a large formation of Ju 87 Stukas was spotted approaching from the west. From the opposite direction came four Bf 109s, and a third enemy gaggle was seen heading southward from over the sea. Middleditch's

Americans look over a captured Ju 87 Stuka dive-bomber of 3./StG 3 found abandoned on a desert landing ground. Parked in the background is Spitfire V 'UF-R' of the RAF's No 601 Sqn (*via Dan and Melinda Shobe*)

flight attacked one of the Bf 109 formations, and he hit an enemy fighter on his first pass, causing it to begin smoking. He then dove behind another Bf 109, but his excessive speed caused his shots to miss the target.

Now at low altitude, and wrestling to regain control of his P-40F ('White 13'), Middleditch got a glimpse of his first victim crashing into the ground before being attacked by three more Bf 109s as he crossed over the coastline. The future ace began turning into their attacks, one by one, firing at them when he had a chance. He hit the first Messerschmitt with a telling burst, and it splashed into the sea.

The other two kept up their attacks, until he was finally able to close in on one of them and hit it solidly in the middle of the fuselage. The fighter half-rolled and then cartwheeled into the water. Now Middleditch only had two guns firing, yet he continued to turn with the last Bf 109 until the German pilot lost his nerve and broke off the combat, allowing Middleditch to return safely to LG 174.

A few weeks later, Maj Gen Lewis H Brereton, Ninth Air Force commander, made a surprise visit to the 57th FG. According to group lore, the unit's personnel were quickly rounded up for a decorations ceremony, in which Lt Middleditch was to be awarded the Distinguished Service Cross in recognition of his combat success. The motley group of desert warriors included cooks in aprons, mechanics in grease-stained coveralls, and even some men stripped to the waist.

Lt Middleditch, who had been helping some mechanics working on a P-40 at the time, hopped down from astride a partially dismantled Merlin engine and took his place in the front row. When the general approached him, he stepped forward and saluted smartly, only noticing later that a roll of toilet paper was protruding from his pants pocket!

In his diary, Gen Brereton indicated that the medal was awarded to Lt Middleditch as the 'first ace' of the Ninth Air Force. An extensive search of 57th FG records has only turned up credits for four enemy aircraft destroyed by Lt Middleditch up to this date, but the general turned out to be correct nevertheless. When the young pilot scored again on 2 April 1943, no one else in the Ninth Air Force had yet reached five victories.

The future leading ace of the 57th FG also scored his first confirmed victory over the El Alamein front. 1Lt Roy E 'Deke' Whittaker, a 23-year-old native of Knoxville, Tennessee, had joined the US Army Air Corps in the Spring of 1941, and earned his pilot's wings just five days after the Pearl Harbor attack. He served as a flight instructor for a short period before joining the 65th FS 'Fighting Cocks' in New England. He saw combat for the first time on 13 August 1942, flying in an RAF Kittyhawk formation that bombed and strafed tents and trucks south of El Alamein.

Lt Whittaker completed his 13th combat mission on the morning of 26 October, escorting bombers and encountering no aerial opposition.

P-40F-1 'White 54' *Margo* of the 65th FS/57th FG had an eventful career before it met this fate. The regular aircraft of Lt Leo B Margolian, the fighter was flown by Capt Tom Clark when he shot down two C.202s on 26 October 1942, and then by 1Lt 'Deke' Whittaker when he scored his second victory – a CR.42 – the following day. Note how the original Olive Drab top camouflage has been revealed by removing the fairings for the P-40's wing and tail (*via Mrs Richard Maloney*)

2Lt Dale R Deniston of the 66th FS/ 57th FG flew this P-40F off the USS *Ranger* to Africa in July 1942. *ROBIN* 'White 84' displays the overall desert tan upper camouflage applied to all of the 57th FG's original Warhawks, along with the word *ZOMBIE* painted on the right wing above its three 0.50-calibre machine guns. Future ace 2Lt R J 'Jay' Overcash scored his first confirmed victory while flying this aeroplane on 28 October 1942 (*Dale Deniston*)

Then at 1425 hrs that same day he was up again in his P-40F 'White 43' *Miss Fury!* when the 65th FS was scrambled to intercept an incoming air raid. Whittaker's flight, led by Capt Thomas W Clark, attacked Italian C.202s south of El Daba and came away with four victories. Capt Clark was credited with two confirmed destroyed, and Lts Whittaker and Robert Metcalf got one apiece.

Whittaker scored again near El Daba the next day during an encounter with Italian Fiat CR.42 biplane fighters, getting one confirmed, one probable and one damaged.

During this period, the 66th FS was separated from its parent group and assigned to the RAF's No 233 Wing, flying out of LG 91. It was from here that 2Lt R Johnson 'Jay' Overcash took off on the morning of 28 October for an escort mission with his squadron, and returned after having notched his first victory. The formation was jumped by Bf 109s, and Overcash knocked one down for his squadron's only claim of the mission. Following a transfer to the 64th FS, Overcash claimed four more victories to reach 'acedom'.

Bombed up and ready to go, P-40F 'White 72' *The Shadow* of the 66th FS/57th FG sits on a desert landing ground. Lt Wade Claxton was its regular pilot (*Lou Lederman*)

This gathering of 64th FS/57th FG officers at LG 174 in October 1942 includes two future aces. These pilots are, from left to right, Lts Donald C Volker, Robert J 'Rocky' Byrne (five victories), William M Ottoway, Peter Mitchell (armament officer), Carl Nelson (intelligence officer), William J Mount (scored the first USAAF victory in the MTO), Fred Ryan (engineering officer), R J 'Jay' Overcash (five victories), Thomas T Tilley (0.25 of a victory), George D Mobbs, (four victories) and future squadron commander Capt Glade 'Buck' Bilby (3.5 victories) (Bill Mount)

A late afternoon mission that same day netted one confirmed victory apiece for 66th FS pilots Capt Raymond A Llewellyn, 1Lt Robert M Adams and 2Lt Thomas M Boulware, who was later killed in action.

The last future ace to claim his first victory during the struggle at El Alamein was 2Lt Robert J 'Rocky' Byrne of the 64th FS. Byrne, a former professional baseball player from St Louis, Missouri, had arrived in Egypt in August to join the 64th.

On 30 October 1942, he was assigned to fly P-40F 'White 13' (the same aeroplane in which Lt Middleditch had scored his three kills on 27 October) on a dive-bombing mission along the coast. With 12 Warhawks of the 65th flying as top cover, Maj Clermont Wheeler led the 64th FS ten miles out to sea before turning south-east toward the target at 13,000 ft. Reaching the coast, Wheeler spotted the building he was assigned to attack and peeled off to begin his bomb run, with his seven Warhawks close behind. The bombs were released at 8000 ft, and none actually hit the target. The Warhawks were then attacked head-on by six Bf 109s.

P-40F-1 'White 74' *???* of the 66th FS/57th FG taxies out at the start of a dive-bombing mission from LG 174 in Egypt in October 1942. The aeroplane also carried a cartoon of a devil on its rudder, along with the inscription *Heil Hell*. The diamond pattern on the nose was a common marking seen on 57th FG Warhawks. 1Lt William E Taylor was flying this aeroplane on 27 October when he received credit with three other pilots for the destruction of a CR.42 (Lou Lederman)

Maj Wheeler and Capt Richard E Ryan snapped off bursts at the leading German fighters as they shot by, getting credit for one damaged and one probably destroyed respectively. Lt Byrne also came under attack and fired at a passing Bf 109, but saw no hits. He then spotted three more Messerschmitts below him and dove to attack them. Closing in behind one and opening fire, Byrne watched as the stricken fighter fell to the desert floor with one wing tearing off as the rest of the wreckage burst into flames. The other Bf 109s fled for safety, and Byrne returned to LG 174.

Not so lucky was 1Lt Gordon Ryerson, who damaged a Bf 109 in the scrap before taking hits in the engine, cockpit and tail section of his P-40F 'White 32'. Wounded in one hand and struggling with damaged controls, Lt Ryerson was only able to make left turns. Somehow, he managed to fly the Warhawk home to LG 174, but the aeroplane flipped over on landing and had to be written off. Lt Ryerson survived the wreck and returned to combat flying, only to later be killed in action.

By 4 November it had become clear to Gen Rommel that the *Afrika Korps* faced destruction if it did not disengage from Montgomery's attack-

Warhawks of the 66th FS/57th FG take off from LG 174 on a bombing mission. The nearest aircraft, 'White 76', was named *Spirit of '76*, and its regular pilot was Lt Ralph M Baker. The second aircraft was Lt Wade Claxton's 'White 72', christened *The Shadow* (*Lou Lederman*)

Lt Gordon Ryerson of the 64th FS/57th FG flipped 'White 32' while landing at LG 174 on 30 October 1942 after a scrap with Bf 109s. 'Babe' Ryerson survived the wreck, but was killed in action just weeks later (*Lyle Custer*)

A crew chief stands on the wing of P-40F-1 'White 60' *TADPOLE* – note the thin outline on the Warhawk's fuselage numbers. 2Lt Charles F Constanzo of the 65th FS/57th FG destroyed a Bf 109 in this aeroplane on 11 January 1943, but he was in turn shot down on the Palm Sunday 1943 'Goose Shoot' mission (*Ed Silks*)

1Lt Gil Wymond of the 65th FS/ 57th FG stands next to the first of some **16** *HUN HUNTERs* **he** would fly in the MTO during the war. The two victory swastikas below the cockpit date this photo of P-40F 'White 46' as November or December 1942. Wymond commanded the 65th FS for two years, from May 1943 through the end of the war in Europe (*Gilbert O Wymond III*)

Col Frank Mears, CO of the 57th FG, demonstrates the use of a new weapon, the napalm firebomb, to his group at LG 3 (Martuba, in Libya) on 23 November 1942. Mears led the 57th off the USS *Ranger* in July 1942, and commanded the group until 23 December 1942, when he was transferred to Ninth Air Force headquarters (*Dale Deniston*)

ing 8th Army at El Alamein. Much to the displeasure of his superiors in Berlin, Rommel ordered his forces to begin an orderly retreat westward. Thus began the next phase of war in 'The Blue' – a 1400-mile chase across Libya and Tunisia that would continue until the following spring.

Rommel, for all his brilliance as a tactician and field commander, had simply not been able to overcome the sheer weight of numbers commanded by Montgomery. Similarly, the vaunted JG 27 collapsed under pressure from Allied aerial attacks. Already depleted in aircraft and experienced pilots at the beginning of the El Alamein campaign after two years of constant combat over the desert, JG 27 was withdrawn from Africa and replaced by JG 77, fresh from the Eastern Front.

During the fighting over El Alamein, pilots of the 57th FG scored a total of 27 confirmed victories, five probables and 12 damaged, while losing just a handful of P-40s. More importantly, they had matured as a combat team and mastered the fighter-bomber tactics of the DAF. Before the end of the North African campaign, the 57th FG would move some 34 times to new airfields as the Allied advance pressed farther west, completing the trek at Cape Bon, Tunisia, in June 1943.

As if the strength of the DAF was not already overwhelming the Luftwaffe and *Regia Aeronautica* units in Africa, new American fighter forces now began joining the fight. As we will see in Chapter Two, the Allied landings in Morocco and Algeria on 8 November 1942 opened a second front in North Africa, and further complicated the defensive challenge facing Axis forces. In addition, two more USAAF fighter groups equipped with P-40s – the 79th FG and later the 324th FG – were sent to Egypt for assignment to the Ninth Air Force. The tide was running in favour of the Allies, but many months of heavy fighting still lay ahead in North Africa.

TORCH TO TUNISIA

In the pre-dawn hours of 8 November 1942, a vast armada of 500 warships and 350 transports converged at several locations off the coastline of north-west Africa and began disembarking troops bound for Casablanca, in Morocco, and Oran and Algiers, in Algeria. This was Operation *Torch*, the opening of a second front on the African continent. Designed primarily to relieve some of the pressure that German forces were applying in the Soviet Union at that time, it had the added benefit of adding a new threat to Rommel's *Afrika Korps* as it fell back from El Alamein toward Tunisia under attack from the British 8th Army.

The Vichy French forces holding Morocco and Algeria – ostensibly Axis allies – put up minimal resistance to *Torch*, capitulating after two days of fighting. Thus, some 1500 miles of North African coastline fell to the Allies, springing the 'back door' to Tunisia wide open. Over the next three weeks, the Allies would land 185,000 troops, 20,000 vehicles and 200,000 tons of supplies for the assault on Rommel's rear.

The American air component of *Torch* was the newly-formed Twelfth Air Force, commanded by Maj Gen James H Doolittle, the famed 'Tokyo raider'. Seven of the Twelfth Air Force's fighter groups were drawn from the growing strength of the Eighth Air Force in England, including three P-38 units, two P-39 units and two units equipped with reverse-Lend Lease Spitfires. An eighth fighter group, the 33rd FG, arrived directly from the United States with the invasion force aboard the aircraft carrier USS *Chenango* (a converted tanker).

Equipped with 77 P-40Fs, the 33rd FG was ordered to fly ashore as soon as the French airfield at Port Lyautey, in Morocco, was secured. As it happened, this area saw some of the stiffest French resistance, which delayed the 33rd FG's arrival until 10 November. Ground personnel of the 33rd, meanwhile, had travelled in the convoy aboard the USS *Anne Arundel*, and came ashore with the troops on the first day of the invasion.

The pilots of the 33rd FG pose with one of their 77 P-40Fs on the deck of the aircraft carrier USS *Chenango* in November 1942, just prior to the Operation *Torch* landings at Port Lyautey, in Morocco. Lt Col William W Momyer, group CO, is standing just to the left of the propeller blade (*John Bent*)

Lt Col Momyer sits in the cockpit of a 33rd FG P-40F, possibly at Port Lyautey. Momyer would score the first of his eight confirmed victories on 4 January 1943 after the group had moved to Tunisia (*Charles Duncan*)

A P-40F-5 of the 33rd FG takes off from the USS *Chenango* on 10 November 1943, bound for Port Lyautey. Note the national flag on the fuselage and the yellow borders on the national insignias – both special markings applied for *Torch* (*National Archives photo via John Bent*)

Leading the 33rd FG was Lt Col William W Momyer, a man particularly well suited for the assignment as commanding officer. Momyer had entered military service in 1938, and completed pilot training the following year. After gaining experience in an operational US Army fighter squadron, he was sent to Egypt in March 1941 to serve as a technical advisor to the RAF, which was then beginning to equip squadrons of the DAF with Lend Lease P-40 Tomahawks. In this capacity, he was not only able to assist the RAF but also to gain valuable insights into combat operations that he would apply later. Returning to the US, Momyer was given command of the 33rd FG in June 1942, and directed the final months of its operational training.

Two days of attacks by US naval aircraft and shelling by ships off shore had left Port Lyautey's runway badly cratered from numerous hits. As a result, the 33rd FG pilots ran into trouble when they attempted to land. One such indivudual was 1Lt Charles H Duncan of the 60th FS. He recalled that seven members of his squadron alone, in addition to the group commander, wrecked their aeroplanes on landing;

'There was simply no place to land. Momyer tried to land short and tore his gear off on the lip of the runway. Norman and Horton both nosed up. I decided that I would try something different, and landed at an angle to the left of the runway, which was an open field with mud like glue. As my aircraft slowed, I gave it full throttle to go around but it slowed more, so I cut the throttle and miraculously stopped without nosing up. It took a tank to pull me out – my fighter suffered no damage, however.

Helmeted groundcrewmen work on a P-40F of the 33rd FG after lifting it back on its wheels following a crash landing, possibly at Port Lyautey, during *Torch* (*Roger White photo via George Dively Jr*)

'The 58th came in the next day and had four accidents – I know not why because the middle crater had by then been filled in. One guy was in his landing roll and we were along the sides of the runway all motioning for him to stop so as not to run into the remaining crater at the end of the runway. He somehow misinterpreted and waved back to us as he slowly ended up in the crater!'

In all, 58 P-40s arrived safely at Port Lyautey. Of the 17 aeroplanes damaged in landings, five were eventually repaired. One P-40 crashed taking off from the carrier, and another simply disappeared. Then the 33rd FG experienced the classic military phenomenon – 'hurry up and wait'. The quick French capitulation left the Warhawk pilots with little to do for the rest of November but fly patrols and stand alert for air attacks that did not come.

Meanwhile, more P-40s arrived on 14 November. USAAF planners, expecting heavy losses in the initial *Torch* assault, had hastily assembled 35 more P-40Fs, and pilots, at Floyd Bennett Field, New York, and sent them on their way to North Africa aboard the British aircraft carrier HMS *Archer*. Led by Maj Philip G Cochran, a colourful character who had

P-40F Warhawks of Detachment J, the so-called 'Joker Squadron', pack the deck of the British aircraft carrier HMS *Archer* on 9 November 1942 while en route to North Africa. The Warhawks, which include 41-14491 and 41-14512, are camouflaged in Dark Earth and Middlestone over Neutral Gray (*George Matuch*)

commanded the 65th FS/57th FG prior to its deployment to Egypt, the thrown-together unit was officially called Detachment J, but soon adopted the name 'Joker Squadron'.

Perhaps due to a lack of time, and to the previous successes in P-40 carrier take-offs, none of the 'Joker Squadron' pilots received any training in carrier operations prior to them leaving port. HMS *Archer*, however, was a small carrier intended for operating Fairy Swordfish biplanes, not slow-climbing P-40s. It was equipped with a compressed-air catapult system that was supposed to give the aeroplanes an additional 70 mph in take-off speed when they reached the end of the deck.

On launch, pilots were instructed to press their head against the P-40's headrest, leave their parachute unhooked and their canopy locked open. This did not inspire confidence in many of the young pilots, including 2Lt Oscar Hearing. As it turned out, his scepticism was warranted;

'Due to the location of my aeroplane on board the carrier, I was the third from last man off. As I was sitting there waiting my turn on the catapult, I noticed that the first 15 or so aircraft had left the deck and continued to climb toward altitude. The second 15 aircraft, however, had left the deck and disappeared from sight (a carrier always launches when the bow of the ship is on the rise from the water) and then gained their altitude farther away from the carrier.

'Due to the torque of the engine, my aeroplane drifted slightly to starboard (right) upon leaving the deck and immediately nosed down into the water because of a lack of flying speed. When I finally surfaced, I was on the port side of the carrier, very close and about half way back. I understand the ship drew approximately 23 ft of water down to the keel, so I was somewhere deeper than that in order for me to pass safely beneath it. To those pilots who have never had to use one, that "Mae West" (inflatable life preserver) really works.'

An American destroyer in the convoy picked up Hearing, and the next day he was transferred to a battleship that was on its way to dock in Casablanca. From there, he made his way north 50 miles to Rabat, where the rest of the 'Jokers' had landed – all except the final two, that is. Again, Oscar Hearing recalls;

'After my aborted take-off, the carrier pulled back out to sea and worked on the catapult. Two days later they made another pass at the coast and fired off the last two aircraft. The last man off the carrier (2Lt Robert P Kantner) was able to get his P-40 about 1 1/2 blocks from the deck before he, too, hit the water due to insufficient airspeed. The carrier was on radio silence, so both his and my accidents were unknown until we arrived with our outfit.'

Hearing was eventually assigned to the 59th FS, and flew throughout the unit's service in the MTO. He then moved with the unit to China and India, before returning to the US in June 1944. Kantner, flying

The P-40F of 2Lt Robert P 'Submarine' Kantner sinks into the Atlantic Ocean on 15 November 1942 after an unsuccessful attempt to take off from the *Archer*. Both Kantner and 2Lt Oscar Hearing had to be fished out of the ocean after the *Archer's* catapult failed to provide enough thrust for their Warhawks to gain flying speed on take-off (*John Bent*)

with the 58th FS, would be credited with one Bf 109 destroyed and one damaged during March 1943.

TUNISIAN GUERRILLAS

Orders moving the 33rd FG to the front arrived in early December. The 58th FS flew to Thelepte on 6 December 1942, thus becoming the first American squadron to operate from an airfield in Tunisia. The 60th FS went first to Youks-les-Bains, Algeria, and on to Thelepte a few days later.

The 59th FS remained at Casablanca for the time being, checking out French pilots of the newly-reformed *Lafayette Escadrille* in P-40s. The 59th FS pilots were disappointed to learn on 20 December that their Warhawks had been transferred to the French unit, and that they would in turn be moving up to Thelepte with just five aircraft.

The action started almost immediately for the P-40 pilots at Thelepte. A small force of American paratroopers had captured the airfield in a surprise attack, and the Germans responded by subjecting the barren plot of land to almost daily air attacks by Luftwaffe fighters and bombers. Among the units joining the assault was II./JG 2, newly-arrived from the Channel front and equipped with the Fw 190 – the first of these superb fighters assigned to the Mediterranean area. The unit soon made its

Pilots of the 58th FS/33rd FG found crude conditions when they moved up to the advanced airfield at Thelepte, in Tunisia, in December 1942. Relaxing next to the operations tent are, from left to right, Lts Harold Wilson, Robert Kantner, John Bland, Curtis Buttorff, Johnnie Haselby and Robert Fackler, Sgt Sepington and Lt Tom Thomas (*John Bland*)

A new German fighter in the shape of the Focke-Wulf Fw 190A appeared in the skies over Tunisia in late 1942. Making its combat debut in-theatre with II./JG 2, under the command of Oberleutnant Adolf Dickfeld, these high-performance fighters gave P-40 pilots fits. This particular example was captured and flown by the 79th FG, this group proving the most energetic of all USAAF fighter units in restoring captured Axis war trophies to airworthiness (*George Trittipo*)

Maj Philip G Cochran, seen here in 1944, led operations at Thelepte as CO of the 58th FS. Cochran's college roommate, Milton Caniff, depicted him as the character 'Flip Corkin' in his popular comic strip 'Terry and the Pirates', which appeared in newspapers nationwide in the US during the 1940s (*Mike Halperin*)

Maj Levi Chase was the top-scoring P-40 pilot in the MTO, with ten confirmed victories. He scored two more kills in March 1945 over Thailand and Burma while serving as CO of the P-51D-equipped 2nd Air Commando Group (*Wes Gray photo via George Dively Jr*)

presence felt. *Combat Digest*, a publication produced by the 33rd FG at the end of the war, described the conditions at Thelepte;

'Upon arrival, personnel immediately dug into their new positions, at first scraping shallow holes in the ground and covering them with shelter halves, later building dugouts and planning rooms, and for other unit functions using five-gallon gasoline tins filled with dirt. Supplies of any kind were almost non-existent – rations, mostly British, were scanty. Parts were obtained by salvaging damaged aircraft, and material was so scarce that empty ration tins were used in repairing aircraft. The work of the groundcrews was constantly disrupted by persistent and sudden air attacks. The frequent attacks . . . necessitated maintenance of continuous daylight patrols.'

Commanding 33rd FG operations at Thelepte was Maj Phil Cochran, who brought some of his 'Joker Squadron' pilots to the advanced base with the first contingent of the 58th FS. Cochran was already well known as the model for character 'Flip Corkin' in the newspaper comic strip 'Terry and the Pirates', which was drawn by his college roommate, Milton Caniff. But Cochran was more than that. He was a natural leader and an innovator who would go on to greater fame in Burma as co-commander of the legendary 1st Air Commando Group.

Cochran wasted no time at Thelepte before unleashing his unit against Axis forces in the Kasserine-Gober-Sousse Triangle. In addition to flying defensive patrols, Cochran's P-40s disrupted the enemy with a series of armed reconnaissance, bombing and strafing missions against troop concentrations, port installations, fuel dumps, bridges, highways and rail traffic. The 33rd FG's first aerial victory occurred on 12 December 1942, when 1Lt Charles B Poillon of the 58th FS shot down a Ju 88 near Youks-les-Bains. The bomber was initially credited to Poillon as a damaged, but was later upgraded to a confirmed victory.

Six days later, the man who soon would become the top P-40 ace in the MTO claimed his first victory. No details of the encounter have been found, but Capt Levi R Chase Jr was credited with one Fw 190 destroyed (although his flight log lists the opponent as an 'Me-109') and 1Lt Hershell L Abbott got another Ju 88. Then on 22 December, Chase and 2Lt Tom A Thomas Jr were flying a two-aeroplane recce mission over Tunisia when they spotted a pair of Ju 88s over the west end of Pichon Pass, in the mountains south of Djeba Bou Dabouse. They quickly pounced on the bombers, which were painted in a camouflage scheme described in their combat report as 'similar to that of P-40s', and downed both of them.

Chase's next score would prove to be one of the more unusual ground kills of the campaign. He and 2Lt James W Gray Jr were flying over enemy-held territory between Gabes and El Guettar on 5 January 1943, when they spotted an apparently undamaged B-17 Flying Fortress being towed along a road. Although they did not know it at the time, the four-engined American bomber had force-landed nearby after becoming lost on a ferry flight to North Africa. Captured by the Germans, the aeroplane was being towed toward a Luftwaffe base when the P-40 pilots found it.

Chase and Gray did not like the idea of the B-17 falling into enemy hands, so they dove earthward with guns blazing and strafed the bomber until it caught fire and burned to a hulk. On returning to base, they were credited with a half share of a ground victory apiece.

In early January 1943, the Luftwaffe stepped up pressure on the Allies' forward air bases in Tunisia and Algeria. By this time, Col Momyer had arrived at Thelepte and assumed command of operations there from Cochran, who remained 58th FS commander. On 4 January, during one of these attacks, the group commander and future ace shot down a Ju 88 for his first confirmed victory.

Maj Cochran, meanwhile, never became an ace, but nevertheless added to his reputation in other ways. Most noteworthy was his mission of 10 January. Acting on an intelligence report, he had his P-40 loaded with a 500-lb bomb and took off alone at 0650 hrs, bound for the enemy held city of Kairouan, in Tunisia.

Arriving over the city, Cochran picked out the Hotel Splendida, which had been identified as housing a German headquarters. He was targeted by light flak from the Arab quarter of the city, but kicked the P-40 over into a dive and dropped his bomb directly on the hotel, causing major damage to the structure. After recovering from his dive, Cochran found an Fw 190 approaching from above and behind. He turned into the attack and opened fire, seeing his rounds hit home before the enemy fighter withdrew. He received credit for one aircraft damaged – his first air-to-air claim. Cochran followed up with two confirmed kills over Thelepte during the next three days to round out his tally against the Luftwaffe.

BIG DAY AT THELEPTE

Enemy attacks continued, meanwhile, peaking on 15 January when Thelepte was raided three times and Youks-les-Bains once. A morning raid yielded a claim of one Fw 190 damaged by the 58th FS. Later in the day, Col Momyer sent out an offensive sweep to respond to the attacks. One of the pilots involved was 2Lt John T Bent, who later recalled the mission as his most memorable combat experience;

'Three of us went to Gabes to "suck up" opposition from a German group stationed there. Several '109s followed us in the sun and dived at us when we were coming in to land in sandy weather at Thelepte. I was only aware of the fighters when one of them came in between me and (1Lt Alton O) "Horse" Watkins. "Horse" was shot down – he bailed out but was wearing only a small parachute, and he couldn't get out of it when he landed. He was dragged along in the high wind and died from his injuries. "Horse" was a wonderful man we could never forget.'

Bent, who had shot down a Ju 88 two days earlier while flying with Maj Cochran, landed safely. He was still on the ground at Thelepte when the next enemy raid came in, consisting of nine Ju 88s escorted by four 'timid' Italian C.202s. This time it was the newly-arrived 59th FS's turn to shine. Two of its P-40s, flown by squadron CO Maj Mark E Hubbard

2Lt John T Bent of the 58th FS/33rd FG, seen here with a P-40F in Norfolk, Virginia, in the summer of 1942, was credited with a confirmed victory when he downed a Ju 88 raiding Thelepte on 13 January 1943 (*John Bent*)

and 2Lt Carl E Beggs, were on patrol over the airfield at 1455 hrs when the enemy bombers approached in a shallow V formation at 12,000 ft, with their escorts some 2000 ft above them. The 59th FS intelligence report takes up the account;

'The enemy dove on the field, and our element followed, catching the formation about 15 miles to the north-east. Maj Hubbard attacked the right side of the formation and Lt Beggs the left. On his initial attack Maj Hubbard destroyed one ship and saw the crew bail out. He attacked another, which he observed land on its belly five miles farther on. At this time, with his guns beginning to function improperly, and with ammunition about gone, he pulled away to return to the field. At this time he saw another '88 pull sharply up, wing over and crash. He had not fired on this aeroplane. During the engagement he did not again see the escorts.

'Lt Beggs, also initially observing the escort of four ships high, dove on the left side of the formation from slightly above and behind. He concentrated his fire on the second bomber from the left of the formation. With his first burst he observed the right motor spout flame and smoke, and saw the aeroplane nose slightly down. Lt Beggs followed him closely, continuing to fire. The ship then began to go down at about 30 degrees from about 500 ft. Debris and smoke continued to fly from the ship. He finally pulled away, guns empty, leaving the enemy at the same angle and about 100 ft from the ground. He believes the aeroplane landed on the right side of the road near a stone building.'

Maj Hubbard was credited with two Ju 88s confirmed destroyed and Beggs got one destroyed – Hubbard would score twice more while flying with the 33rd FG. After a spell of leave in the US, he returned to combat in England with the Eighth Air Force's 20th FG. On 18 March 1944, shortly after assuming command of the 20th FG, Hubbard downed 2.5 Bf 109s over Germany to reach ace status. Unfortunately, he also was shot down on that mission and spent the rest of the war as a PoW.

The 59th FS was not finished on 15 January with the victories of Hubbard and Beggs, however, for two P-40s, flown by Capt B Boone and 2Lt Robert H Smith, were also able to scramble during the bombing attack. Here again is another extract from the 59th FS intelligence report;

'Capt Boone and Lt Smith took off at 1455 hrs as bombs were falling on the field. Capt Boone reports seeing ten Ju 88s leaving the field to the north-east. As he approached, the enemy was flying about five or ten feet off the ground. He attacked the rear ship in the middle of the formation. The enemy, when hit by his fire, slid to the right and crashed into the bomber on its right. Both ships fell and burned.

'Capt Boone then made attacks on the right side of the formation, shooting down the farthest ship to the right. He then took the next ship and also shot it down, seeing it crash. With his ammunition expended, Capt Boone broke away to return to the field. He reports three remaining bombers as he broke off the attack.

'Lt Smith, approaching with Capt Boone, attacked a ship in the middle of the formation. He reports opening fire at extreme range and continuing until the '88's rudder was shot off and it crashed. Lt Smith, having expended his ammunition, returned to base.'

The 33rd FG was awarded a Presidential Unit Citation for its defence of Thelepte on 15 January. With four destroyed on the day, Capt Boone immediately became the 33rd FG's top scorer, and appeared likely to become the unit's first ace as well. This was not to be, however, for Boone was shot down and killed just over two weeks later. Ironically, Lt Smith was killed in action on the same day.

Meanwhile, the apparent loss of eight Ju 88s on 15 January temporarily took the starch out of the Luftwaffe's campaign against Thelepte, giving the 33rd FG a much-needed break from the enemy attacks. The group, now down to just 30 operational P-40s, continued to harass Axis ground forces in Tunisia through to the end of the month, but scored no further victories until 31 January. On that day, Maj Levi Chase, now serving as CO of the 60th FS, downed a Bf 109, and damaged a second one, near Gafsa.

February 1943 started with a bang for the 33rd FG, and again the 59th FS did all the shooting. A formation of 12 P-40s, led by Maj Mark Hubbard, went out on 1 February to provide air cover for ground troops near Maknassy, where a tank battle was under way. Turning for home, the Warhawk pilots spotted a Bf 109 flying off to their left. Four P-40s briefly gave chase, but when a large formation of 35 Ju 87s, with 17 Bf 109 escorts, appeared directly in front of the remaining P-40s, the American pilots directed their attention towards the dive-bombers. The Bf 109 escorts attempted to intervene, and a big scrap ensued.

The 33rd's tally for the day was four Stukas and one Fw 190 destroyed, plus two dive-bombers probably destroyed and four damaged. In return, three P-40s were lost.

The top-scoring Warhawk pilot of the day also was one of those shot down – future ace Capt John L Bradley. Leading the third flight, he gave chase to the initial Bf 109 when it was spotted and then turned back with his wingman to confront the main formation of Stukas. Bradley picked out a Ju 87 on the extreme right flank and opened fire, watching as it burst into flames and crashed. He then attacked the last aeroplane on the other side of the formation, and its pilot bailed out as the Stuka went down.

Bradley was just lining up on his third victim when his P-40F-20 (probably 41-19944) was hit by fire from one of the escorts. Smoke filled the cockpit and then the engine quit, forcing Bradley to take to his

It so happened that the four 33rd FG pilots who reached ace status also served as unit commanders. Pictured here in the spring of 1943 are, from left to right, Maj Mark E Hubbard, 59th FS (6.5 victories), Col William W Momyer, 33rd FG (8 victories), Maj Levi R Chase Jr, 60th FS (12 victories) and Maj John L Bradley, 58th FS (5 victories) (*Charles Duncan*)

New P-40L-1 42-10448 makes a low pass down the runway at El Kabrit, in Egypt, in February 1943. This aeroplane was destroyed in a crash on 18 August 1943 whilst serving with a undisclosed unit (*Howard Levy*)

parachute. He landed safely ten miles south of Maknassy and hitched a ride back to Thelepte, arriving there at dusk.

More action was in store the following day, when six P-40s of the 59th FS and four P-39s of the 92nd FS/81st FG ran into a formation of Stukas and Bf 109s near Senna Station while on a recce mission. As with the previous day, the American fighters concentrated their attacks on the Stukas, but this time the escorts were much more effective. Five of the six P-40s failed to return, while only one Stuka was destroyed, credited to Lt Howard J Hutter.

By this time, the 33rd FG had become the most experienced fighter outfit in the Twelfth Air Force, but it had also taken a beating. Now down to just 13 flyable aircraft, and with its roster of pilots diminished as well, the 33rd FG was pulled out of Thelepte on 8 February. Three days later the surviving pilots arrived at Agadir, in Morocco, for a well-earned rest and re-equipment with new P-40Ls. Some of their replacement aeroplanes were transfers from the 325th FG, which had arrived in North Africa via an aircraft carrier in mid-January, but would not commence combat operations until April.

ROUND TWO

Rested and replenished with new aircraft, the 33rd returned to Tunisia in late March 1943 after a stop at Berteaux, in Algeria, for about two weeks. While the group was away from the front, Rommel had unleashed a daring armoured thrust through the Kasserine Pass, with the goal of cutting the Anglo-American army in Tunisia in half. American losses were heavy, and the base at Thelepte changed hands before two divisions of American reinforcements arrived to turn back the *Afrika Korps*, and commence the final phase in the struggle for North Africa.

The 33rd FG flew several missions during its brief stay at Berteaux, and on one of them the unit gained its first ace. The mission of 15 March 1943 was a 36-aeroplane escort of B-25s attacking the airfield at Mezzouna, in Tunisia. Enemy fighters rose to defend the base, and in the fight that developed, three of them went down and four were damaged. Maj Levi Chase, now the CO of the 60th FS, was credited with one victory over a C.202. This was his fifth confirmed kill, making him the 33rd FG's first ace, and therefore the first Warhawk ace in the Twelfth Air Force.

The 33rd FG's new home in Tunisia was Sbeitla, a base so recently vacated by the Luftwaffe that it was still littered with booby traps when the Warhawks arrived on 23 March. Located north-east of Thelepte, and beyond the Kasserine Pass, Sbeitla again placed the 33rd FG in close proximity to the frontline.

Col Momyer immediately threw his P-40s back into the fight, scheduling three missions on 24 March – the 33rd FG's first full day at Sbeitla. The morning mission was an escort for B-25s attacking an enemy airstrip near Djebal Tebeta. A gaggle of Bf 109s hurriedly took off from the strip as the formation approached the target, and Capt John Bradley, who was leading the escort, and Capt Charles Duncan broke away for a diving attack as the enemy fighters were still climbing. Bradley knocked down one of the attackers before the P-40s rejoined the formation.

The Bf 109s kept coming, however, eventually following the P-40s back to Sbeitla, but losing three of their own to Lts Lassiter Thompson, Johnnie Haselby and Harold Wilson along the way. Duncan takes up the story as the P-40s reached Sbeitla;

'They followed us back to Sbeitla and disrupted our landing. In the middle of things Lt Robert Kantner (my wingman) and I started to land because of low fuel. Kantner's coolant was shot out, and he bellied in. On my landing roll I looked back to see a '109 coming down the runway intent on putting me out of commission. I went around, flaps and all, turning and "washing clothes" (pushing the stick every which way and kicking rudder to throw him off). No hits. I decided to slow up and wait for awhile.

'I then saw an Me-109 on the tail of what turned out to be John Bradley's P-40. I was 90 degrees to their flight path, so I pointed my nose at Bradley, and somewhat above, with the intent of scaring off the '109 with my tracers. I had little chance of hitting the '109, and knew I had no chance of hitting Bradley with no lead. I fired a bunch of rounds and the '109 broke off.

'Now, really low on fuel, I climbed to about 5000 ft to throttle back and wait things out. Next I observed a '109 being chased in a climb by two P-40s. The P-40s didn't have enough power or speed to reach the '109. I dived all the way to ground level and zoomed upward to close on the '109, the pilot of which apparently thought he was in no danger. When almost on top of the '109 I fired – but only two or three rounds because that was all I had left. A puff of smoke came from the '109 as he was hit, and his reflexes apparently caused him to pull his throttle to off. I had a time "S-ing" to keep from overrunning him, and he glided in and crashed straight ahead. An engineering unit situated near to where the aircraft crashed, notified our group that the top of the pilot's head had been blown off.'

Later on the morning of 24 March, the 59th FS flew a sweep back over Djebal Tebeta and encountered opposition over the target. Maj Mark Hubbard, squadron CO, claimed one Bf 109 destroyed. One of the pilots involved in the scrap was Lt Richard E Holcomb, who was credited with one Bf 109 damaged. He remembers;

'Lt Harry Haines and I ended up in a ground-level dogfight right over the German airbase. It was quite a fight, as we were out-turning them and shooting up aeroplanes on the ground while they climbed to start the fight again. We would run for home until their cannon shots came close to Harry's tail, and again we would out-turn them. I felt sure at least two were damaged as they left the fight, but we couldn't confirm them.'

Bad weather slowed operations at Sbeitla for several days, but on
29 March the 58th and 60th FSs combined to claim seven Bf 109s

destroyed and five damaged at a cost of just one P-40. More success came on 30 March, when 36 P-40s from all three squadrons escorted B-25s to the enemy airfield at La Fauconniere. This time, the 33rd FG's score was eight confirmed, six probables and four damaged. Among the pilots scoring that day was 2Lt Donald J Wirth of the 58th FS, who had arrived in North Africa with the last batch of carrier-delivered P-40s in February. He wrote this account of the fight nearly 57 years later;

'I was flying my third mission on 30 March. Our flight of four P-40s was flying high cover, 6000 ft above the bombers, when about six Me-109s showed up above us and attacked our flight. We all broke, and as a '109 sailed past me, I reversed my turn and got a good shot at him. The problem was another '109 was behind me, and his cannon shells were getting damned close. I broke hard to the left, stalled and spun out. I recovered from the spin and noticed that the Me-109 was coming in again. I pulled my aeroplane in hard again and lost the '109.

'In the fracas I had lost the other P-40s and the B-25s. To top it off, my engine was now running poorly, so I hit the deck and headed for home. I kept checking for the '109 I had lost contact with, but he was nowhere to be seen. My objective now was to get back to our side of the lines before my engine gave out, as it was threatening to do. I passed a trench full of German soldiers at an altitude of about 50 ft, and they were as surprised to see me as I was to see them.

'The engine was now shaking badly. I knew I had to set the aeroplane down, and very soon, when I saw a nice green "field" ahead with two L-5s parked next to it. There was a lot of smoke next to the "field", and I went through it on my final approach, dropped my landing gear, full flaps, cut the ignition switch and hit the ground. I also hit some camouflage nets and a slit trench where some GIs were dug in. The "field" I had picked to land on was an American artillery position that was covered with camouflage nets. The L-5s were using a road next to it for take-offs and landings.

'The P-40 slid to a stop. The landing gear was knocked back into the wing wells, and I was sitting over a slit trench with some GIs under the aeroplane looking up at me. A warrant officer in the trench invited me to come down and sit with him and the troops, which I did.

'The enemy was shelling the area, and I could hear the explosions, and now knew where that smoke was coming from. When we got a chance, we made a run for the commander's headquarters. It was a rather large GI tent dug in approximately four feet below ground level, with excavated dirt stacked up around it. When we went in, the warrant officer introduced me to Gen Patton and several other officers. They seemed a little perturbed because I had wrecked some of their camouflage.

'Gen Patton said, "What the hell do you want?" I replied that I just wanted to get back to my squadron. Gen Patton replied, "Then get in that god damn Jeep and get the hell out of here". So I left.

'Gen Patton's driver dropped me off at the base at about 1500 hrs. The first person to greet me was Maj Bradley, the squadron CO. He shook my hand and said, "Where's the rest of your flight?" I was so surprised. I thought I was the last one to get back. Later I found out that one pilot belly-landed in a minefield, one bailed out and it took him four days to walk back, and one was captured. The one in the minefield had to wait several days for the engineers to clear a path through the field.'

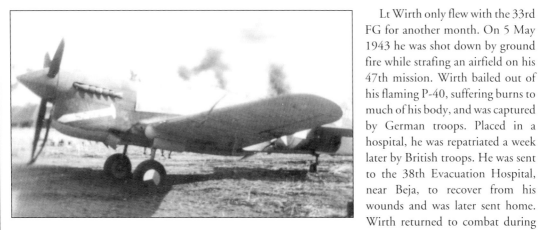

A tarp protects the canopy area of Col Momyer's parked P-40L-5 at Paestum, in Italy, as shells burst in the background. The aircraft's distinctive *SPIKE* nose art is clearly visible, as is the yellow diagonal tail stripe signifying its assignment to the 60th FS and its broad yellow wing bands. Finally, note the fighter's painted hubcaps (*Dr John Woodworth photo via George Dively Jr*)

Col Momyer straps into his P-40L-5 42-10658 for a mission in the late Summer or early Autumn of 1943. Barely visible is the large *SPIKE* nose art and the eight yellow victory swastikas unusually placed just forward of the red-bordered national insignia. The red, white and blue segments decorating the hubcaps are also clearly visible (*Gordon Delp*)

Lt Wirth only flew with the 33rd FG for another month. On 5 May 1943 he was shot down by ground fire while strafing an airfield on his 47th mission. Wirth bailed out of his flaming P-40, suffering burns to much of his body, and was captured by German troops. Placed in a hospital, he was repatriated a week later by British troops. He was sent to the 38th Evacuation Hospital, near Beja, to recover from his wounds and was later sent home. Wirth returned to combat during the Korean conflict, flying F-86s with the 51st Fighter Interceptor Wing (FIW) in 1951-52.

On 31 March, Col William Momyer became the 33rd FG's second ace and, for the time being, its top scorer. On that day he was leading 36 P-40s, each carrying four 20-lb fragmentation bombs, sent to attack a motor park at El Guettar. The Warhawks bombed and strafed successfully, and were then set upon by Bf 109s on the way home. Eight Messerschmitt fighters and one P-40 went down in the fight that ensued. The P-40s split and headed for home, but Momyer then spotted 18 Ju-87s north of the target area and downed four of them, taking his tally to eight.

The colonel continued as CO of the 33rd FG throughout its entire assignment in the MTO, returning home when the unit was transferred to India in early 1944. He had no further opportunities to add to his score, however.

Momyer's scoring lead lasted just four days, for Maj Levi Chase tied him on 1 April by downing two Bf 109s near El Djem airfield. Then, on 5 April, Chase was back in action again when the 33rd FG returned to El Djem with 48 P-40s, the fighters escorting B-25s sent to attack the field. One of the pilots taking part in the mission was Lt Kenneth B Scidmore of the 60th FS, who remembers;

'I was the alternate pilot who followed the mission flight for a brief time, so if anyone had aeroplane trouble I would fill his position. As it turned out I filled in as wingman for Maj Levi Chase, our CO. The mission was targets of opportunity. It was overcast, and we flew over the clouds. After an hour's flight we saw no Me-109s or other targets, so we turned to go home.

'Maj Chase spotted a hole in the overcast and advised the flight that we would descend through the hole. Much to our surprise, we came down right over a German airfield, and right in front of us was an Me-109. Maj Chase fired one burst of 0.50-calibre machine gun fire and the Me-109 blew up. At that moment another Me-109 came across in front of us from the right side. Here was my chance. Flying wing and holding my position, I prepared to fire when again Maj Chase fired one burst and the Me-109 exploded.

'As we crossed the German airfield I saw a P-40 making a belly landing just off the end of the field. It turned out to be Lt Jack Mann. Later we received a card from the Red Cross stating that he was a prisoner in Germany. Many years later I saw him at a 33rd FG reunion.'

Maj Chase's two victories, both confirmed by Lt Scidmore, gave Chase the scoring lead for good. He claimed no further victories before completing his combat tour, but he was credited with hitting a ship while dive-bombing on his last mission, 25 May 1943. Maj Chase's score of ten destroyed and one damaged made him the top American ace in the MTO at that time, and the top MTO P-40 ace of the war. He returned to combat in 1945 as commanding officer of the 2nd Air Commando Wing in Burma, destroying two Japanese aircraft before the war ended. Chase made a career of the USAF, commanding the 8th Fighter Bomber Group during the Korean War and the 12th Tactical Fighter Wing in Vietnam. He retired as a major general.

By 14 April the frontline had shifted deeper into Tunisia, and the 33rd FG moved to a new base at Ebba Ksour. From there, the group kept up a steady pace of bombing and strafing missions into the shrinking Axis-held territory, hitting the cities of Bizerte and Tunis, along with airfields, highway traffic and other targets of opportunity. The group had few chances for further air combat before the German and Italian forces in North Africa surrendered on 13 May 1943.

ENTER THE 325th

The second P-40 outfit to join the Twelfth Air Force was the 325th FG, which had flown 72 P-40s off the USS *Ranger* to Cazes airfield, near Casablanca, on 19 January 1943. The group was barely six months old, having formed in July 1942 as a unit of the Boston Air Defense Wing. It boasted a strong cadre of leaders, however, including Lt Col Gordon H Austin, group CO and a survivor of the Pearl Harbor attack, and Maj Robert L Baseler, executive officer and a future ace.

After suffering the initial disappointment of having to turn over half of its P-40s to the 33rd FG in February, the 325th rebuilt its strength while flying training and convoy-cover missions from Tafaroui, in Algeria. Combat veterans, including Maj Phil Cochran of the 33rd FG, were brought in to conduct lectures that helped the green pilots learn the finer points of aerial warfare. Finally, on 5 April 1943, the 325th FG got orders to move two of its squadrons to the frontline airfield at Montesquieu, in Algeria, about 100 miles east of Tunis. The 318th and 319th FS moved immediately, but the 317th FS remained behind for a month while its complement of P-40s was brought up to full strength.

The 325th FG flew its first official combat mission on 17 April 1943, when 36 P-40s provided escort for B-25s assigned to attack Mateur. Over the target, a pair of Bf 109s came diving through the 325th's formation, and one of them shot down the P-40 flown by Flt Off Howard T Cook of the 318th FS. The young pilot survived the encounter and was picked up by British troops, who returned him to Montesquieu. The mission was

Lt Col Gordon H Austin, CO of the 325th FG, led his unit off the carrier USS *Ranger* to Casablanca on 19 January 1943, and commanded the group until the following August. Seen here in his 'White 44' P-40L-5 42-10664, nicknamed *Lighthouse Louie*, Austin scored two victories before being transferred to command a B-26 medium bomb group (*via Dwayne Tabatt*)

otherwise uneventful, but later the 325th FG would look back and realise that it was the first of 59 consecutive escort missions flown by the group in which no bombers were lost to enemy fighters.

The eighth mission flown by the 325th FG, on 29 April, marked its first experience with dive-bombing, and then on 6 May the group recorded its first aerial victories. The assignment that day was a sea sweep from Cape Bon to Cape Serrat, with 12 P-40s of the 318th FS carrying 500-lb bombs and 12 of the 319th providing escort. Several vessels were attacked and left burning before the formation turned for home.

One flight of four from the 319th became separated from the main formation on the return flight. By chance, they came across a landing strip and noticed about 20 German Ju 52/3m transport aeroplanes parked there. Diving to the attack, 1Lt Harmon E Burns spotted a Ju 52 flying at 1000 ft over the water north-east of Protville. He gave the transport several bursts from his machine guns and then watched as it became engulfed in flames and splashed into the sea.

Meanwhile, 1Lt Frank J 'Spot' Collins became separated from the other three P-40s and set course for home. He flew a short distance before spotting a Bf 109 flying with its wheels down, obviously in a landing approach. Collins slipped in behind the enemy fighter, closed to point-blank range and opened fire. The stricken fighter fell to the ground and burst into flames. This was the first of nine victories Collins would score in P-40s and P-47s with the 325th FG.

The 325th FG had completed 20 missions by 13 May 1943 – the date of the Axis surrender in North Africa. And although it was one of the last fighter units to reach the MTO, the 325th was already showing promise, and it would quickly mature into one of the leading P-40 outfits during the summer months ahead.

This P-40F-5 was the first Warhawk assigned to 2Lt Warren F Penney of the 317th FS/325th FG. 'White 31's' nickname (*BAD PENNY*)refers to the old saying 'a bad penny always comes back'. This machine also featured a triangle design on its hubcaps. Penney would score two confirmed victories in P-40s and two more in 1944 after the 325th FG had converted to P-47s (*via Dwayne Tabatt*)

P-40F-15 'White 34' (41-19841) was assigned to the 317th FS/325th FG, and it is shown here in Tunisia in the spring 1943, prior to the application of the 325th FG's famous checkertail markings (*Edward Oroukin photo via Dwayne Tabatt*)

OUT OF AFRICA

There was a buzz around the camp at LG 174 on 2 November 1942, and the ever-present flies weren't causing it. Pilots of the 57th FG were talking about the new, but familiar, face in camp – that of Lt Col Peter McGoldrick. Many of the men knew McGoldrick from more peaceful days, for he had led the 66th FS as CO from August through to October 1941, and had then gone to 57th FG headquarters as operations officer. Here, he had remained until shortly before the group departed the US for Africa. At that time, the 30-year-old West Pointer had been named commander of the recently-formed 79th FG, with instructions to prepare the group for combat operations as quickly as possible.

Now Lt Col McGoldrick returned to the 57th FG, but this time as a visitor. While his 79th FG ground personnel were travelling to Egypt via military transport ships, and his pilots were busy ferrying new P-40s from the assembly plant at Accra to airfields near Cairo, McGoldrick and several of his key subordinates had attached themselves to the 57th FG to gain combat experience. Just as the 57th FG pilots had gained their first combat experience with battle-hardened RAF squadrons the previous summer, so now their counterparts from the 79th FG would get their first taste of aerial warfare while flying on the wings of American MTO combat veterans.

Sadly, Peter McGoldrick's first taste of combat would also be his last. On 9 November 1942 he took off with five other P-40s to strafe a German convoy that had been reported near Charing Cross, in Egypt. When they arrived over the target, the Warhawks were met with heavy ground fire from the convoy. Nevertheless, the P-40 pilots made two strafing passes over the target, causing considerable damage.

On the second pass over the convoy, McGoldrick's P-40 was seriously damaged by return fire. He turned away from the target and nursed the ailing Warhawk eastward toward friendly territory. Finally, the engine gave up and he picked out an open space for a forced landing. McGoldrick had no way of knowing that he had chosen to land the aeroplane in a minefield. As the P-40 touched down, it struck a mine and the explosion demolished the fighter, killing Lt Col McGoldrick.

The death of Peter McGoldrick touched the men of the 57th and 79th FGs deeply, but there was no time to dwell on such matters. Gen Rommel's *Afrika Korps* was now in full retreat in Western Egypt, and the DAF was throwing everything it had at the German and Italian forces. As the front moved steadily westward, the Allied fighter units followed closely behind in order to

Most pilots of the 79th and 324th FGs ferried new P-40s across Africa from the assembly plant at Lagos, in Nigeria, to depots near Cairo, prior to entering combat operations. Here, Shell Oil Company employees refuel a P-40 at Fort Lamy, in French Equatorial Africa, which was one of the regular stops on the ferry route (*W D Gatling*)

Equipped with a mix of British and American vehicles, an advanced party of the 66th FS/57th FG moves up to a new base in Libya during the winter of 1942-43 (*Dale Deniston*)

keep their aircraft within range of their targets. Less than a week sfter McGoldrick's death, the 57th FG had already moved twice, and was now beyond the Egyptian border, operating from the landing ground at Gambut, in Libya.

The complex logistics involved in moving the squadrons fell on the shoulders of the hard-working ground personnel. Borrowing again from RAF tactics, each American squadron divided into A and B groups. Both groups consisted of enough mechanics and armourers to keep the squadron operational. While A Group was servicing the P-40s, B Group would move forward to the next base and prepare it for operations. Then when the P-40s moved to B Group's location, A Group would go yet farther forward, and the process would begin again.

One of the men who took part in these leap-frog operations was Sgt Lyle Custer, an armourer in the 64th FS. On 9 November 1942 he made this diary entry;

'Today we went on another 100 miles closer to the front. There were a lot of wrecked German tanks and trucks, and a few dead bodies, along the road. Saw a lot of wrecked aeroplanes on airdromes, most of them German but a few British. There are a lot of minefields. Some of the towns we went through were B-El Arab and Daba. Most of the towns are only piles of stones. We saw lots of enemy prisoners, mostly Italians but some Germans. As we neared our field they said there were snipers, so we had to have our rifles ready. We reached our field in the afternoon. Lots of Lockheed Hudsons flew in. Two enemy aeroplanes flew over. The ground is so hard that we cannot dig a fox hole – there are large stones under the ground.'

Meanwhile, the three squadrons of the 79th FG moved into the 57th FG's old home at LG 174 on 19 November 1942 to commence the final phase of its operational training under the new CO, Lt Col Earl E Bates. The new group commander was a highly experienced pilot, having won his wings in 1935, and had been serving as operations officer at the time of McGoldrick's death. From LG 174, groups of pilots would move forward to fly with the 57th FG until the full group was ready to begin independent operations. It was one of these pilots, 1Lt Samuel L Say of the 85th FS, who on 8 December 1942 drew first blood for the 79th FG 'Hawks'.

The mission flown on the 8th was typical of the period. Twelve P-40Ks of the 64th FS (three flown by 85th FS pilots) were assigned to bomb the enemy airfield at Marble Arch, in Libya, with top cover provided by 12 Warhawks of the 65th FS. The P-40K, which was relatively new to the unit, was an Allison-powered version of the Warhawk that had begun

1Lt Samuel L Say of the 85th FS was credited with the 79th FG's first air combat claim when he damaged a Bf 109 on 8 December 1942 while flying on attached duty with the 57th FG. He scored two confirmed victories during his 80-mission combat tour, returning home with the rank of captain (*Tom Anderson*)

arriving in November to replace the 57th FG's ageing and depleted ranks of P-40Fs.

Performance of the two models was roughly similar. The P-40K was considered slightly faster at low levels, but its engine only provided full power up to about 15,000 ft, while the Merlin-powered P-40F's operational ceiling was about 5000 ft higher. The 57th FG was the only

As losses of P-40Fs mounted in the 57th FG, the group began to receive P-40K Warhawks as replacements in November and December 1942. These aircraft were powered by the Allison engine, which limited their combat effectiveness to an altitude of about 15,000 ft. This factory-fresh aircraft was photographed at Heliopolis, in Egypt, prior to its assignment to a 57th FG squadron (*Howard Levy*)

USAAF unit to fly P-40Ks in the MTO, operating them through the spring of 1943 until more Merlin-powered P-40s became available in-theatre.

The formation, led by Capt Richard E Ryan of the 64th FS, approached the target at an altitude of 5500 ft under an overcast sky. Several Bf 109s were seen taking off from the airfield a few minutes before the P-40s released their bombs, and these enemy fighters made an aggressive attack as soon as they reached sufficient altitude. Capt Ryan got a shot at one of them on the first pass, as did Lt Say, who saw smoke pouring from his victim as it dove for the deck. He was unable to follow, however, and claimed the aircraft as damaged.

Claims of two aircraft destroyed apiece were confirmed for 1Lt George Mobbs and 2Lt Steven Merena of the 64th FS, plus 1Lt Arnold Jaqua of the 65th FS. One further victory went to 1Lt William S Barnes of the 64th FS. Despite his two scores, this was another tough mission for Lt Mobbs, who wrote this account of it;

'I was flying P-40K "White 11" on that mission. I had gotten good shots at two different '109s during the fight. Because of the intensity of the fight, I hadn't observed the final results of the first one (which Merena confirmed). The second one was in a downward spiral and I tried to watch it down. This lack of caution led to my problem. Suddenly holes started to appear in my left wing. It seemed to take a long time for me to realise what was happening. I started a tight turn and moved into a position to retaliate, but when I pulled the trigger nothing happened. My guns wouldn't fire. I also realised I was now alone.

'I started trying to make headway toward our lines, hoping to get to friendly territory in case I had to go down. It was difficult to make progress. As soon as I would head toward home I was attacked. I then observed that there were two above, two on my left and two above to my right. Two from one side would make a pass, I would turn into them, and then the two from the other side would make a pass.

'In an attempt to make better progress, I thought I would turn into them only to the point that I could see the cannon hole in the '109's nose spinner – then maybe they wouldn't be leading me enough, and I could make more progress toward home. Somewhere in here I took a hit in the left fuselage and took a fragment in my left thigh. Although I have a clear recollection of the thoughts I had as to how to thwart their efforts to shoot me down, the sequence of those efforts is vague in my memory. I know that somewhere in there I thought my chances were so slim that when turning into them I thought I would try to ram.

The squadrons of the 57th FG began painting their unit badge on the noses of their P-40s in December 1942. *Pretty Baby* displays the 'Black Scorpion' of the 64th FS, plus a nicely rendered flying pin-up girl. Note also the star painted onto the hubcap. Unfortunately, the regular pilot of this aeroplane is not known (*Dale Deniston*)

'I felt that the German anti-aircraft gunners helped me in my plight, because in shooting at me they were also getting close to the '109s. Eventually the fighters broke off, either because they were out of ammunition or low on fuel or both. I made it back to our landing strip and belly-landed – a very rough belly landing. My trim tabs were ineffective, probably damaged by gunfire, and I was exhausted.

'If you look closely at the Me-109 you will note that there is a hole in the spinner for the cannon. There is also a protrusion on the left side of the engine cowling about the size of an old-fashioned stovepipe. These are two images that I saw frequently in my dreams after that day.'

George Mobbs continued to fly in the 64th FS through to August 1943, scoring four confirmed victories and achieving the rank of major.

Little more than a month after this engagement, the 57th FG passed the Marble Arch, Mussolini's monument to himself on the boundary between Cyrenaica and Tripolitania, on the way to its next airfield. The 79th FG, meanwhile, remained in reserve at LG 174, enduring frequent dust storms and other miseries of life in 'The Blue' while it waited to join the fight.

This new P-40F-1 (41-14295) of the 87th FS/79th FG was photographed at El Kabrit, in Egypt, on 29 January 1943 while the group was in training. Notable is the two-tone uppersurface camouflage, which was factory-applied on late production P-40F-1s bound for North Africa, and the aeroplane-in group number 'White X90'. The 79th FG used the prefix 'X' to distinguish its aircraft from those of the 57th FG. Note also the application of a red prop spinner and an RAF fin flash – both standard markings of the DAF (*Howard Levy*)

Warhawks of the 85th FS/79th FG 'Flying Skulls' await their next mission at Causeway LG, in Tunisia. In the foreground is 'White X15', which was regularly flown by Lt Charles K Bolak, Next in line is Lt Sammy Say's 'X21', and behind it is 'White X32', which 2Lt Milton Clark used to shoot down a C.202 on 7 June 1943 (*Chet Campbell photo via James V Crow*)

On 20 January, more than 100 trucks of the 79th FG finally rolled out of LG 174 and headed west into Libya. The group stopped at landing grounds for various intervals, but it remained in reserve until finally arriving at Causeway LG, in Tunisia, on 13 March. Here, on the following day, the 79th FG flew its first mission as an operational unit within the DAF's No 211 Group.

——— CONFRONTING THE MARETH LINE ———

In the three months following the 8th Army's breakout at El Alamein, Montgomery's troops had chased the *Afrika Korps* some 1400 miles across Egypt and Libya. With the capture of Tripoli on 23 January 1943, Montgomery paused to regroup and replenish his forces. Ahead of him in southern Tunisia stood the Mareth Line, Rommel's seemingly impenetrable defensive position running from the Gulf of Gabes to the Dahar and Matmata Hills to the west. Beyond the hills lay the barren wastes of the Dahar and past that the Grand Erg Oriental sand desert.

Built by the French prior to the war to protect its Tunisian colony from the Italians in Libya, the Mareth Line consisted of steel and concrete fortifications and an underground communications system. When Rommel's forces reached the line in late January, the respite allowed by Montgomery gave the *Afrika Korps* time to add tank traps, minefields, gun emplacements and miles of barbed wire. Luftwaffe fighters of JG 77 were stationed close behind the line on airfields at Zuara, Bir Toual, Gabes and El Hamma. Any frontal assault on the Mareth Line was bound to be a costly, bloody affair.

February 1943 was a relatively quiet time for the USAAF fighter squadrons in Libya, as most of the aerial action involved Twelfth Air Force aircraft over Tunisia in connection with Rommel's thrust through Kasserine Pass. In March, the DAF began in earnest the process of softening up the Mareth Line. It was on one of these missions that 1Lt Edward H Ellington of the 65th FS/57th FG had a frightening but memorable experience. He recounted;

'We were on the deck strafing in the Medinine area when I took a 20 mm shell in the wing, which caused a huge hole. I broke for the coast and stayed on the deck until I was certain I was behind friendly lines. When I cut in I was well behind our own landing strip and came upon a British P-40 re-supply unit.

'When I landed the British sergeant took a look at my bird and said, "Damn, Yank. You've got a problem there". I can't remember his exact words, but the paraphrase is pretty close. The aeroplane was gushing gas from its ruptured tanks, and you might say that I had had a lucky day, since I was damned fortunate not to have run out of gas over the sea.

'The amusing thing about this incident was that the sergeant then

1Lt Edward H 'Duke' Ellington of the 65th FS/57th FG, standing centre, poses with his groundcrew and their P-40F, 'White 61'. The pilot is flanked by armourer Bill Hahn to the left and crew chief Fernando Royball to the right. The man kneeling is unknown. Note the swirl pattern on the hubcap (*Edward Ellington*)

said, "Yank, do you want another aeroplane?" I hadn't realised that this was a re-supply outfit, but naturally I was eager to get back to my strip. So I jumped at the chance, even though this aeroplane's cockpit was configured for British use, and was somewhat different from ours.

'By now it had been several hours since I had left my revetment at my home strip. They all knew I was missing. My appearance, taxying into my own revetment with a new aeroplane after taking off on a mission in my old one, was hard to explain.'

One of the original pilots who had flown off the USS *Ranger*, Ellington extended his combat tour in the 65th FS and flew 116 missions before returning home in September 1943. He rejoined the 65th FS in November 1944, and was serving as squadron CO when the war ended. Ellington completed 180 combat missions in World War 2, and stayed in the USAF until 1968, when he retired with the rank of colonel.

On 13 March 1943, the 57th FG experienced its most spirited engagement with enemy fighters in many weeks. The mission was a fighter sweep to the Gabes area, with 36 P-40s of all three squadrons participating. Several of the pilots flying in the 64th FS were members of the newly-arrived 324th FG, the third American P-40 unit assigned to the DAF. Pilots of the 314th FS/324th FG had been assigned to the 57th FG to gain experience, while others from the 316th FS would soon commence operations with the 79th FG.

The formation flew from the 57th FG's base at Ben Gardane out over the sea, and then turned in across the coastline just north of Gabes. Heavy anti-aircraft fire bracketed the 64th FS, which was flying at low altitude. Then the formation was attacked by Bf 109s, and a huge dogfight erupted. One of the P-40s was hit immediately, and it dove out of the formation towards the shoreline but was not seen to land. This was probably the aircraft flown by Capt John Simpson, a flight leader in the 314th FS who was flying his first combat mission and was taken prisoner, spending the rest of the war in captivity.

Two pilots from the 66th FS, which was flying top cover, recorded their memories of this battle. First, 2Lt John E Teichrow;

'On my 22nd mission, 13 March 1943, our squadron was attacked by approximately 25 Me-109s. The total flight lasted about one hour and forty-five minutes, and was a typical free-for-all melee. I recall firing, instinctively, at a '109 as he flew in front of me and I saw pieces of his rudder and elevator flying off. He never saw me – I couldn't hit the side of a barn with a handful of sand.'

1Lt Dale Deniston of the 66th FS recorded the same day's action in his diary;

'What a terrific day. Only training flights in the morning. I took a wonderful bath and had a change to clean clothes. At 2.00 pm we went out on a fighter sweep to the Gabes area. The 64th Squadron with 12 aircraft leading, 65 Squadron with 12 aircraft middle cover, and 66th

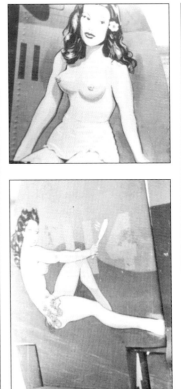

The talents of Cpl Joseph Pumphrey were legendary in the Ninth Air Force. A bespectacled armourer in the 85th FS/79th FG, Pumphrey decorated the rudders of many squadron P-40s with pin-up paintings that rivalled the quality of noted magazine artist Varga (*both Robert Duffield*)

One of the pilots flying top cover on the mission of 13 March 1943 was 2Lt John E Teichrow, who was credited with one Bf 109 damaged in that day's air battle. The 324th FG suffered two losses that day whilst making its combat debut (*via Dan and Melinda Shobe*)

One of the pilots downed on 13 March 1943 was Maj Robert F Worley, the popular CO of the 314th FS/324th FG. He was fortunate to belly-land his P-40F-1 behind enemy lines unhurt and escape back to Allied territory. The aeroplane, which was retrieved after the battlefront had moved past it, carries the 324th FG prefix 'Y.' In Ninth Air Force units, numbers 10, 40 and 70 were normally assigned to the COs of the three squadrons within the group (*Howard Levy*)

A pilot of the 314th FS/324th FG taxies P-40F-1 41-14221 at El Kabrit in February 1943. This aircraft was condemned to salvage on 28 April 1943 (*Howard Levy*)

Squadron top cover. I was in tip top cover in Jim Curl's section, him leading. I led an element, with Charlie Leaf as my wingman. Near Gabes, at 18,000 ft, we were attacked by 15-plus Me-109s and Macchi 202s.

'God! What a fight followed. I got in a fair firing burst. Lost from my formation, I flew all over the place – aeroplanes swirling thick as flies. I saw one hit the water below. We have four pilots missing, none from our squadron. It was the longest and fiercest fight I've ever been in. Lasted at least 20 minutes. Maj Worley of the 314th shot down but is safe.'

Lts Teichrow and Deniston were each credited with one Bf 109 damaged. Confirmed victories were awarded to 1Lt William S 'Tommy' Beck of the 64th FS, 1Lts Thomas Boulware, John Gilbertson and Thomas T Williams of the 66th FS and Maj Archie Knight, 57th FG operations officer, who also scored two Bf 109s damaged. Lt Robert Douglas of the 64th FS was shot down to become a PoW, and Lt W E Jenks of the 64th was also lost.

This was an unsettling combat debut for the 324th FG, much like the 79th FG had experienced. Maj Robert F Worley, mentioned in Deniston's diary entry, was the popular CO of the 314th FS. He was fortunate to belly-land his P-40F-1 'White Y10' behind enemy lines unhurt and then avoid capture to return to his unit, which he would continue to lead for many months to come. Like many of his fellow pilots, Worley made the USAF a career. He rose to the rank of major general, but on 23 July 1968 he was killed in action when his RF-4C Phantom was hit by ground fire and crashed near Da Nang Air Base, South Vietnam.

The 324th FG was just at the beginning of a long and distinguished combat career in the MTO. Formed from a cadre of 33rd FG officers at Philadelphia, Pennsylvania, in early July 1942, the group was commanded by Lt Col William K 'Sandy' McNown. After the normal training period in the US, the 324th FG departed for overseas duty on 1 November 1942. The pilots of the 314th and 315th FS were flown to Lagos, in Nigeria, where they picked up new P-40s that they would ferry to Egypt, just as the 79th FG's pilots had done earlier. Meanwhile, the ground personnel were en route via ship. Most of the pilots made several ferry trips while waiting for the rest of the group to arrive, then spent the first two months of 1943 in training on bases in Egypt.

The 314th and 316th FSs flew as additional units of the 57th and 79th FGs, respectively, during the Tunisian campaign. The group's third squadron, the 315th FS, had provided many of the pilots for Maj Phil Cochran's 'Joker' Squadron (see Chapter 2), so it remained in the US temporarily to rebuild its strength, before following the others to North Africa. Finally, all three squadrons were reunited as the 324th FG in June 1943 and continued to operate as such through to the end of the war.

ASSAULT ON TUNISIA

The first mission of the 79th FG as a frontline unit was an uneventful escort of B-25s attacking the Mareth Line on 14 March 1943. Flak was fairly heavy and accurate over Zarat, and 1Lt Sammy Say notched another first for the 79th FG when he picked up several pieces of shrapnel in the wing of his Warhawk. Daily missions followed, and on 21 March the 79th FG claimed its first confirmed aerial victory when 1Lt Asa A Adair of the 87th FS knocked down a Bf 109 while escorting B-25s over the Mareth Line.

On that same day, the 8th Army finally opened its offensive into Tunisia. Montgomery's plan for confronting the Mareth Line should not have fooled the Germans, for they had used similar flanking tactics against France's Maginot Line in 1940, but it did. He split the 8th Army, using three divisions for a frontal assault on the line near the seacoast, while the New Zealand Corps swept to the west in a flanking movement through the Matmata Hills toward El Hamma. Meanwhile, the American II Corps advanced on Gafsa from the west.

The *Afrika Korps*, now under the command of Gen von Arnim, had no choice but to withdraw northward from the Mareth Line toward Cape Bon. As Gen Montgomery told his troops, 'The Axis is caught like a rat in a trap'.

Fondouk fell to American troops on 28 March, and the 8th Army passed Gabes three days later. Although Axis forces were again in retreat, the fighting was far from over in Tunisia. Indeed, it would take the combined forces of Montgomery and Eisenhower another two months to achieve total victory in North Africa. During that period, the P-40 units of the Ninth Air Force would continue to pound away at ground targets, and take on the Luftwaffe and *Regia Aeronautica* at every opportunity.

In the early afternoon of 2 April 1943, Capt Lyman Middleditch of the 64th FS/57th FG led eight P-40Ks out of Soltane LG for an armed reconnaissance mission covering the coastal highway along the Gulf of Gabes. As the formation crossed the bomb line at 10,000 ft, Middleditch spotted about 20 Bf 109s flying northward from the Gabes area. Obviously, the Messerschmitt pilots had seen the P-40s as well, for they climbed slightly, then turned left into the sun and dove from 11,000 ft at the American fighters.

Capt Middleditch had been watching the Bf 109s all this time, and was not surprised in the attack. He turned his formation into the diving fighters, and soon the sky became a mass of swirling aeroplanes. As was often the case in these circumstances, both sides' pilots were so busily engaged in looking for targets while avoiding their opponents that they found it difficult to get off a shot. In this case, Capt Middleditch was the only P-40 pilot who had a chance to open fire, shooting off 300 rounds into a passing Bf 109.

Then, as quickly as the engagement had began, it was over. Middleditch reformed his eight P-40s and led them back toward their base, dodging a barrage of heavy flak on the way. Later, Middleditch described the fight that made him an ace;

'We spotted some 20-plus Me-109s, which came in to attack – rather hesitantly, I thought. Things didn't look too good at first, but their hesitation gave us time to get set. They probably thought we were baiting them with a small formation, since we'd had things so much our way during the past few days.

'After a few minutes of manoeuvring, one of the Jerries made a pass at me. He was a little late in pulling out. I saw my tracers go into his wing root and some pieces flew off the right wing. Then I noticed a few "golf balls" float by my prop and I knew that some of Jerry's friends were on my tail. I quit my victim and went into a spin to evade. It worked. But I missed the opportunity to see the aeroplane I'd hit go into the deck. The ground forces later confirmed the crash.'

2Lt Andrew A D'Antoni of the 314th FS/324th FG taxies a P-40F-1 (possibly 'White Y31') across a desert landing ground in early 1943. The aeroplane carries a yellow diamond – the 314th FS insignia – on the cowling. One of his squadron's original pilots, D'Antoni shot down a C.202 on 4 July 1943 for his only confirmed victory (*Andrew D'Antoni*)

Capt Middleditch did not claim the Bf 109 he hit as being destroyed, because the 64th FS sortie report lists enemy casualties of just one Bf 109 damaged. Apparently the claim was upgraded to a confirmed destroyed when later evidence came in. Be that as it may, the Ninth Air Force acknowledged its first ace six days after the scrap, crediting Middleditch with five victories. The 28-year-old New Yorker completed his combat tour in July 1943 and returned to the US, where he spent the rest of the war in Training Command.

———— 'A HUGE GAGGLE OF GEESE' ————

Of all the missions flown by P-40s in the MTO, none stands out so clearly as the 57th FG's late afternoon show of 18 April 1943, dubbed the 'Goose Shoot' by the participating pilots, but soon upgraded by the press corps to the moniker 'Palm Sunday Massacre'.

On that single mission, Warhawk pilots of the 64th, 65th, 66th and 314th FSs were credited with destroying no fewer than 74 German aircraft during a 20-minute engagement over the Gulf of Tunis, losing just six of their own. In addition, four pilots joined the Ninth Air Force's list of aces that day.

It should come as no surprise that such a lopsided victory took place in the closing days of the Tunisian campaign. As the Axis forces squeezed tighter and tighter into the Cape Bon area, it became clear to them that their cause was lost. For several weeks before Palm Sunday, large formations of Luftwaffe transport aeroplanes had been shuttling back and forth between Cape Bon and Sicily.

Initially, the primary purpose of these flights was to carry reinforcements and war material to North Africa – later they began evacuating troops. Considering the air superiority enjoyed by the Allies over Tunisia, it was just a matter of time before the shuttle flights began to run into trouble. In encounters on 10 and 11 April off Cape Bon, P-38s of the Twelfth Air Force had shot down 50 Ju 52/3m transports, and it was also reported that American B-25 medium bombers on a shipping sweep over the Mediterranean had downed a number of Junkers transports with their turret guns.

In the early hours of the morning on 18 April, intelligence reports reaching the 57th FG headquarters at El Djem indicated that the Germans were planning a big airlift of key personnel from Tunis to Sicily. Col Art Salisbury, CO of the 57th FG since December 1942, duly began sending out patrol missions during the day, but time after time they returned to base with nothing to report.

With hope of a big score fading, Col Salisbury laid on the final mission of the day in co-ordination with No 244 Wing RAF – 48 P-40s from his four units, with a top cover of No 92 Sqn Spitfires IXs for a maximum effort patrol flown before dark. (*text continues on page 59*)

Capt James G Curl, CO of the 66th FS/57th FG, led the famed Palm Sunday 'Goose Shoot' of 18 April 1943, claiming three of the 74 victories credited for the mission. Curl left the squadron shortly after the mission, but returned to combat in late 1944 as CO of the 2nd FS/52nd FG, flying Mustangs in Italy. Sadly, he was killed in action on 19 March 1945 (*via Dan and Melinda Shobe*)

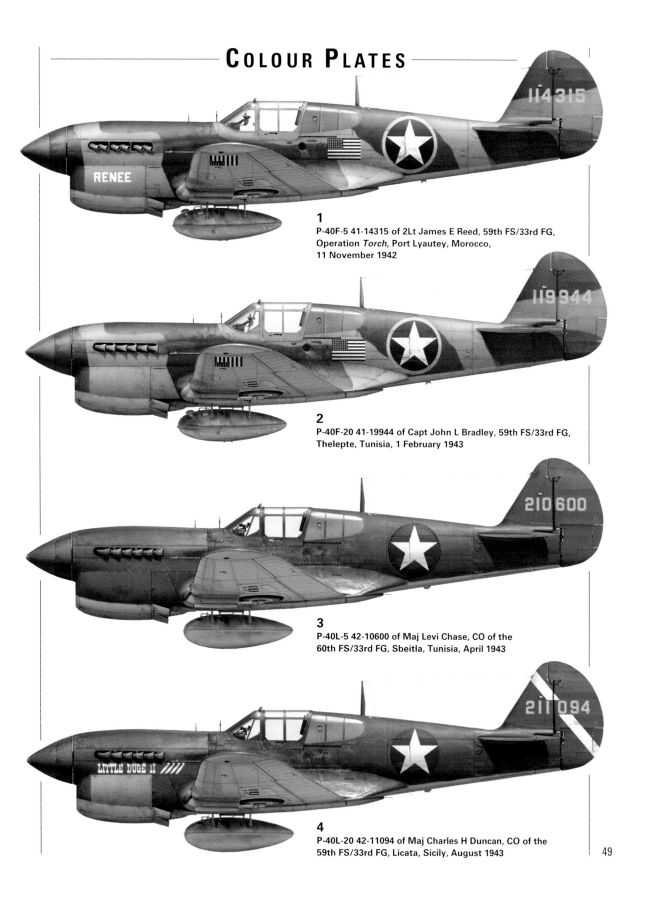

1
P-40F-5 41-14315 of 2Lt James E Reed, 59th FS/33rd FG,
Operation *Torch*, Port Lyautey, Morocco,
11 November 1942

2
P-40F-20 41-19944 of Capt John L Bradley, 59th FS/33rd FG,
Thelepte, Tunisia, 1 February 1943

3
P-40L-5 42-10600 of Maj Levi Chase, CO of the
60th FS/33rd FG, Sbeitla, Tunisia, April 1943

4
P-40L-20 42-11094 of Maj Charles H Duncan, CO of the
59th FS/33rd FG, Licata, Sicily, August 1943

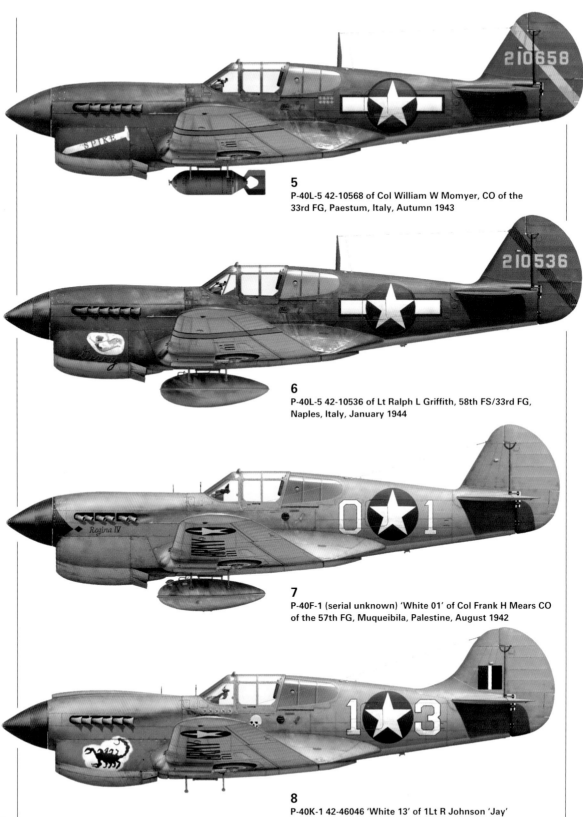

5
P-40L-5 42-10568 of Col William W Momyer, CO of the
33rd FG, Paestum, Italy, Autumn 1943

6
P-40L-5 42-10536 of Lt Ralph L Griffith, 58th FS/33rd FG,
Naples, Italy, January 1944

7
P-40F-1 (serial unknown) 'White 01' of Col Frank H Mears CO
of the 57th FG, Muqueibila, Palestine, August 1942

8
P-40K-1 42-46046 'White 13' of 1Lt R Johnson 'Jay'
Overcash, 64th FS/57th FG, Hani Main, Tunisia, May 1943

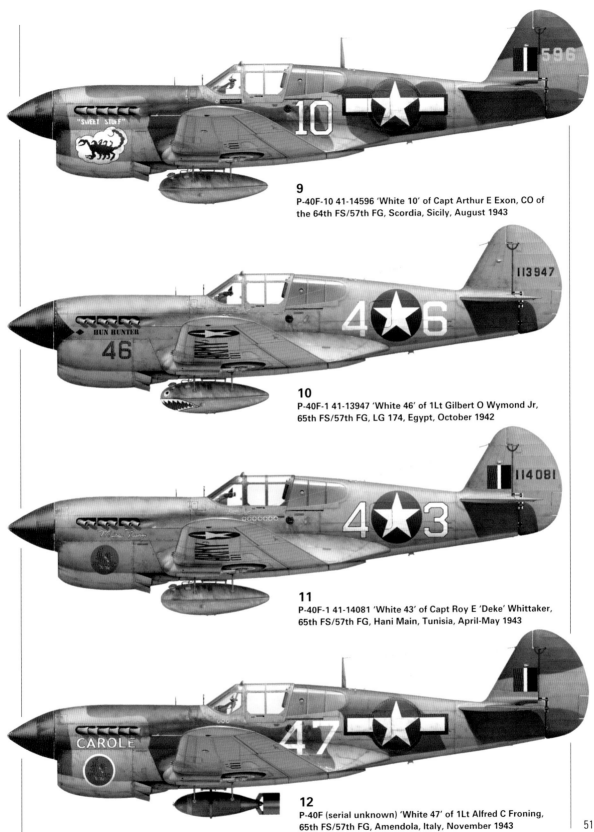

9
P-40F-10 41-14596 'White 10' of Capt Arthur E Exon, CO of the 64th FS/57th FG, Scordia, Sicily, August 1943

10
P-40F-1 41-13947 'White 46' of 1Lt Gilbert O Wymond Jr, 65th FS/57th FG, LG 174, Egypt, October 1942

11
P-40F-1 41-14081 'White 43' of Capt Roy E 'Deke' Whittaker, 65th FS/57th FG, Hani Main, Tunisia, April-May 1943

12
P-40F (serial unknown) 'White 47' of 1Lt Alfred C Froning, 65th FS/57th FG, Amendola, Italy, November 1943

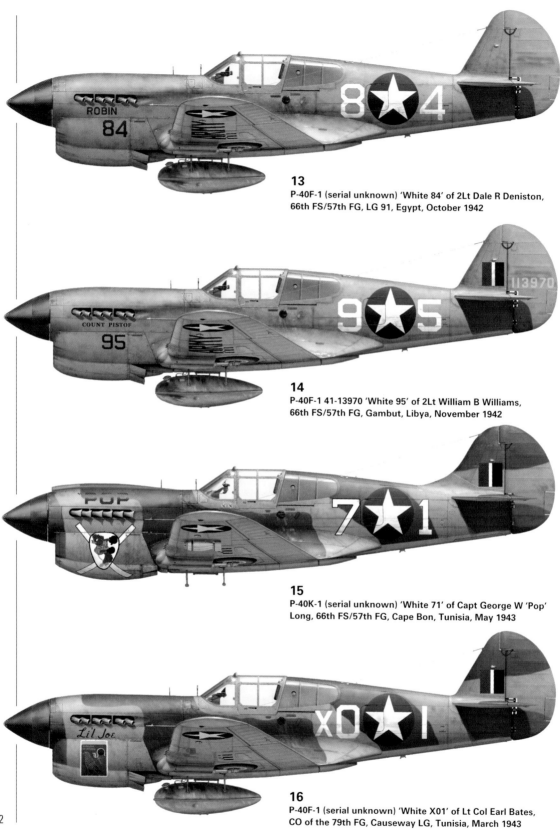

13
P-40F-1 (serial unknown) 'White 84' of 2Lt Dale R Deniston,
66th FS/57th FG, LG 91, Egypt, October 1942

14
P-40F-1 41-13970 'White 95' of 2Lt William B Williams,
66th FS/57th FG, Gambut, Libya, November 1942

15
P-40K-1 (serial unknown) 'White 71' of Capt George W 'Pop'
Long, 66th FS/57th FG, Cape Bon, Tunisia, May 1943

16
P-40F-1 (serial unknown) 'White X01' of Lt Col Earl Bates,
CO of the 79th FG, Causeway LG, Tunisia, March 1943

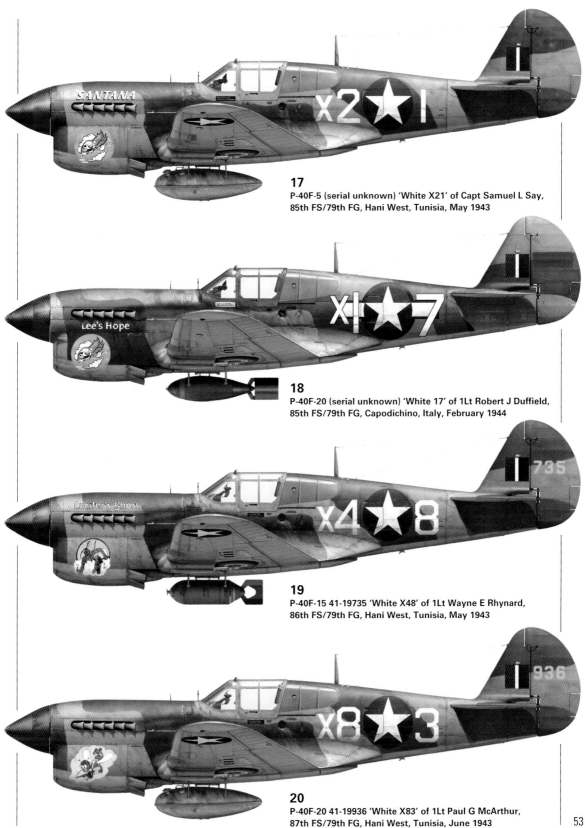

17
P-40F-5 (serial unknown) 'White X21' of Capt Samuel L Say,
85th FS/79th FG, Hani West, Tunisia, May 1943

18
P-40F-20 (serial unknown) 'White 17' of 1Lt Robert J Duffield,
85th FS/79th FG, Capodichino, Italy, February 1944

19
P-40F-15 41-19735 'White X48' of 1Lt Wayne E Rhynard,
86th FS/79th FG, Hani West, Tunisia, May 1943

20
P-40F-20 41-19936 'White X83' of 1Lt Paul G McArthur,
87th FS/79th FG, Hani West, Tunisia, June 1943

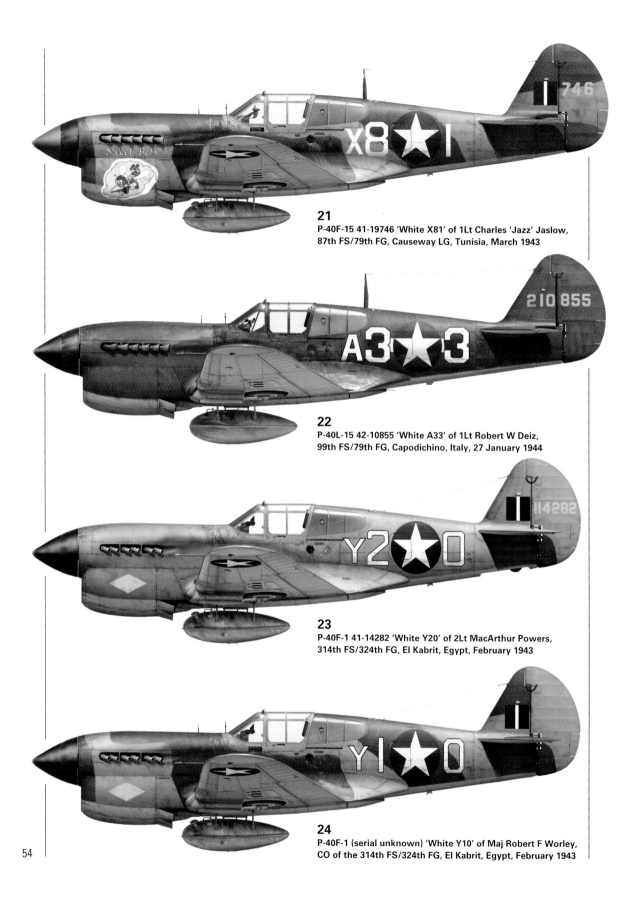

21
P-40F-15 41-19746 'White X81' of 1Lt Charles 'Jazz' Jaslow,
87th FS/79th FG, Causeway LG, Tunisia, March 1943

22
P-40L-15 42-10855 'White A33' of 1Lt Robert W Deiz,
99th FS/79th FG, Capodichino, Italy, 27 January 1944

23
P-40F-1 41-14282 'White Y20' of 2Lt MacArthur Powers,
314th FS/324th FG, El Kabrit, Egypt, February 1943

24
P-40F-1 (serial unknown) 'White Y10' of Maj Robert F Worley,
CO of the 314th FS/324th FG, El Kabrit, Egypt, February 1943

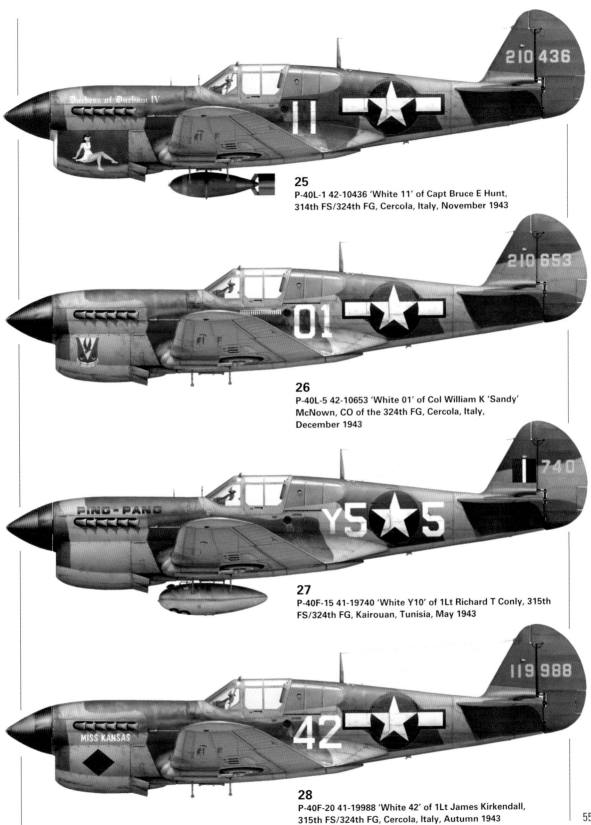

25
P-40L-1 42-10436 'White 11' of Capt Bruce E Hunt,
314th FS/324th FG, Cercola, Italy, November 1943

26
P-40L-5 42-10653 'White 01' of Col William K 'Sandy'
McNown, CO of the 324th FG, Cercola, Italy,
December 1943

27
P-40F-15 41-19740 'White Y10' of 1Lt Richard T Conly, 315th
FS/324th FG, Kairouan, Tunisia, May 1943

28
P-40F-20 41-19988 'White 42' of 1Lt James Kirkendall,
315th FS/324th FG, Cercola, Italy, Autumn 1943

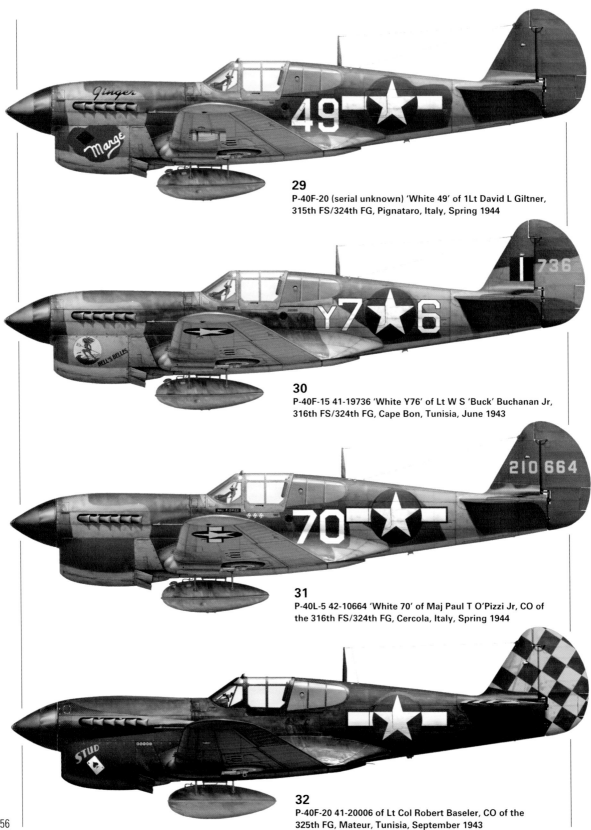

29
P-40F-20 (serial unknown) 'White 49' of 1Lt David L Giltner, 315th FS/324th FG, Pignataro, Italy, Spring 1944

30
P-40F-15 41-19736 'White Y76' of Lt W S 'Buck' Buchanan Jr, 316th FS/324th FG, Cape Bon, Tunisia, June 1943

31
P-40L-5 42-10664 'White 70' of Maj Paul T O'Pizzi Jr, CO of the 316th FS/324th FG, Cercola, Italy, Spring 1944

32
P-40F-20 41-20006 of Lt Col Robert Baseler, CO of the 325th FG, Mateur, Tunisia, September 1943

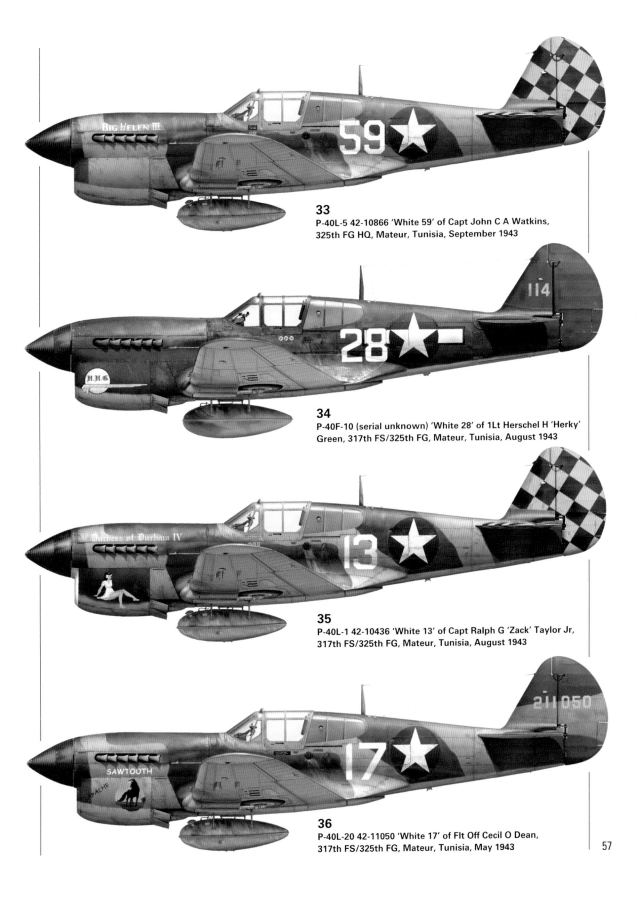

33
P-40L-5 42-10866 'White 59' of Capt John C A Watkins,
325th FG HQ, Mateur, Tunisia, September 1943

34
P-40F-10 (serial unknown) 'White 28' of 1Lt Herschel H 'Herky'
Green, 317th FS/325th FG, Mateur, Tunisia, August 1943

35
P-40L-1 42-10436 'White 13' of Capt Ralph G 'Zack' Taylor Jr,
317th FS/325th FG, Mateur, Tunisia, August 1943

36
P-40L-20 42-11050 'White 17' of Flt Off Cecil O Dean,
317th FS/325th FG, Mateur, Tunisia, May 1943

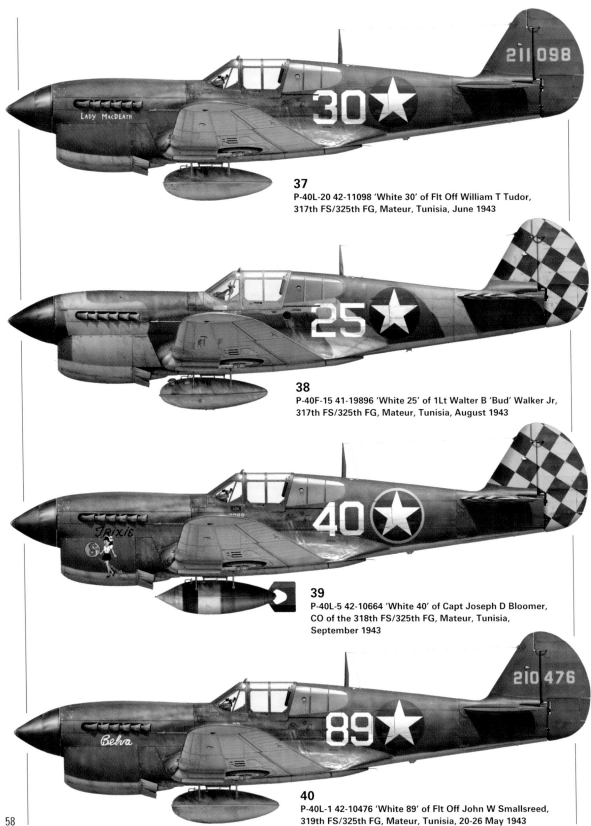

37
P-40L-20 42-11098 'White 30' of Flt Off William T Tudor,
317th FS/325th FG, Mateur, Tunisia, June 1943

38
P-40F-15 41-19896 'White 25' of 1Lt Walter B 'Bud' Walker Jr,
317th FS/325th FG, Mateur, Tunisia, August 1943

39
P-40L-5 42-10664 'White 40' of Capt Joseph D Bloomer,
CO of the 318th FS/325th FG, Mateur, Tunisia,
September 1943

40
P-40L-1 42-10476 'White 89' of Flt Off John W Smallsreed,
319th FS/325th FG, Mateur, Tunisia, 20-26 May 1943

Capt G W 'Pop' Long, commander of A Flight within the 66th FS/57th FG, destroyed two Ju 52/3ms during the 18 April 1943 'Goose Shoot' – the only victories of his long tour of duty in North Africa. His P-40K, 'White 71', like him, was nicknamed *POP* because Long's wife gave birth after he arrived overseas. His was one of the few P-40Ks known to have carried Dark Earth/Middlestone camouflage on its uppersurfaces (*via Dan and Melinda Shobe*)

As far as can be determined, 2Lt Richard E Duffy of the 314th FS/324th FG only encountered enemy aircraft on one mission, but he made the most of the opportunity. He was credited with destroying five Ju 52/3ms and damaging a Bf 109 over the Gulf of Tunis during the 'Goose Shoot' of 18 April 1943 to become 'an ace in a day' (*via Bruce Hunt*)

P-40s began lifting off from El Djem at 1705 hrs, led by Capt James G 'Big Jim' Curl, a highly experienced flight leader with the 66th FS.

Capt Curl led the Warhawks northward, with his 66th FS in low position and the other units stacked above to the 64th FS on top. Two P-40s dropped out with engine trouble and returned to base. After picking up the Spitfires for tip-top cover, the remaining 46 Warhawks skirted the coast from Sousse to Nabual. Then Curl turned northwest and crossed Cape Bon before heading over the Gulf of Tunis under an overcast sky.

With the light beginning to fade, Curl turned the formation around and headed back south from about six miles offshore. Then, as if by magic, there appeared before Curl a huge formation of tri-motored transport aeroplanes flying in a 'V-of-Vs' formation low over the water. There was no time to count, but he later estimated seeing close to 100 aeroplanes below him. Curl glanced briefly back over his shoulder to ensure the Spitfire escorts were in place, then ordered the Warhawks to attack.

Curl's squadron, at the bottom of the formation, and the 314th FS in low cover position were closest to the transports and made first contact. The medium cover 65th FS followed them in, but the 64th FS and the Spitfires above were attacked by Bf 109s that were escorting the transports. Capt Curl described his view of the engagement for a Ninth Air Force publication;

'When I first saw the Jerry aeroplanes they were right beneath us, about 4000 ft down. Camouflaged as they were with green colouring, it was rather difficult to distinguish the transports against the sea. When we got near they looked like a huge gaggle of geese, for they were travelling in perfect 'V' formation, tightly packed. The boys simply cut loose and shot the daylights out of them.

'What concerned our pilots most was the danger of hitting our own aircraft, for the concentration of fire was terrific and the air was totally filled with whistling and turning machines. There were cases of pilots missing the transport they aimed at and hitting the one behind. It was as fantastic as that – you just could not miss.

'There was no real fighter opposition because the British Spitfires that were flying our top cover did a

2Lt MacArthur Powers of the 314th FS/324th FG and another pilot make a low pass over an airfield in Egypt, in early 1943. A future ace, Powers transferred to the USAAF after scoring 2.25 victories flying Spitfire VBs for the RAF with No 145 Sqn during 1942. His P-40F-1 (41-14281, 'White Y20') displays the serial number in yellow on its rudder and the squadron's yellow diamond on its cowling. Powers named his aeroplanes *Jessy*, but no photos of the application on this aircraft have been found (*Howard Levy*)

If Powers' pass wasn't low enough, how about this buzz job by a pilot of the 87th FS/79th FG at Cape Bon, in Tunisia. The pilot's identity is unknown . . . perhaps for obvious reasons (*George Trittipo*)

grand job in keeping the Messerschmitts so busy that they could not interfere with our attack to any extent.'

Capt Curl was credited with two Ju 52/3ms and one Bf 109 destroyed, plus two Ju 52/3ms damaged. Promoted to major and given command of the 66th FS shortly thereafter, he completed his first combat tour in August 1943 and returned to the US. He came back to the MTO in late 1944 to command a Mustang squadron in the 52nd FG, but was killed in action on 19 March 1945.

Three pilots attained the unusual status of 'ace in a day' on 18 April by destroying five aircraft. One of them, 2Lt Arthur B 'A B' Cleaveland of the 66th FS, downed five Ju 52/3ms, but was so excited when he got back to El Djem that he dug in the wingtip of his P-40 on landing and wrecked his aeroplane. Another pilot credited with five of the transports was 2Lt Richard E Duffy of the 314th FS. Describing his attack on the Ju 52/3ms, he said;

The centre two in this quartet of 314th FS/324th FG pilots accounted for eight confirmed victories in the 18 April 1943 rout off Cape Bon. 2Lt MacArthur Powers (second from left) was credited with four Ju 52/3m transports and a single Bf 109 destroyed, while 1Lt Edward L Stout (second from right) claimed three Junkers transports. Neither Lts 'Dan' D'Antoni (left) nor Roger Woodard were scheduled to fly on the mission (*Andrew D'Antoni*)

Capt Roy E 'Deke' Whittaker of the 65th FS emerged from the 19 April 'Palm Sunday Massacre' as the all-time top-scoring ace of the 57th FG. His four confirmed victories that day boosted his total to seven kills, which he displayed boldly on the fuselage of his P-40F-1 (41-14081, 'White 43') *Miss Fury* . . . (*Roy Whittaker Jr*)

. . . although the ranking ace was not at the controls of his assigned machine on the 19th. Instead, he got stuck into the Ju 52/3ms flying the 57th FG's most colourful P-40F, Col Art Salisbury's 'White 01'. As this photograph of the aircraft's nose clearly reveals, this machine (whose serial remains unknown) was decorated with all three unit badges – it is believed that this trio of markings also appeared on the starboard side of the Warhawk as well

'They were so tightly packed that I had three in my sights at the same time. I even got two with one burst. Those two collided and fell into the sea. The next one also crashed into the water with its engines smoking, and the other two were flamers.'

Then there was 2Lt MacArthur Powers of the 314th FS, who destroyed four Ju 52/3ms and one Bf 109. While Duffy was a relatively green combat pilot, Powers was an old hand. He had left his native Inwood, New York, in 1941 to join the Royal Air Force. After earning his wings as a sergeant pilot in March 1942 and flying briefly with No 91 Sqn on the Channel Front, he transferred to Egypt and joined No 145 Sqn flying Spitfires. Powers downed 2.25 Bf 109s with No 145 Sqn before transferring to the USAAF in January 1943. He gave this brief description of the fight;

'There were so many good targets in the air and crashing onto the deck, and so many of us after them, I was afraid I was going to be left out. We almost fought among ourselves to get to the enemy.'

Capt Roy Whittaker, a highly experienced flight leader in the 65th FS, already had three victories to his credit and added four more on 18 April. He recalled the fight for a reporter;

'I attacked the JU-52s from astern at high speed and fired at two aeroplanes in the leading formation. The bursts were short and the only effect I saw was pieces flying off the cabin of the second ship. I pulled away and circled to the right and made my second attack. I fired two bursts into two more '52s – again in the leading formation. They both burst into flames. The second flew a little distance and then crashed into the water. I lost sight of the first and didn't see it hit. I then made a third pass and sent a good burst into the left of the formation, at another Junkers. As I pulled away, it crashed into the water. By that time the Me-109s were among us.

2Lt Alfred C Froning of the 65th FS/ 57th FG scored the first two of his eventual six confirmed victories during the 18 April mission. He is seen here with his crew chief some time after scoring his third victory on 30 April 1943. Note the inscription *HOT LIPS* above the wing guns of his P-40 'White 47', named *Carole*. Froning scored his final three victories after the 65th FS had transitioned to P-47s (*Ed Silks*)

As I pulled up to the left, I saw a '109 dive through an element of four Warhawks, and I tagged on his underside and gave him a long burst in the belly. He crashed into the sea from a thousand feet.

'I then joined up with some Warhawks which were "lufberrying" with six Me-109s. I met one of these fighters with a quartering attack and hit him with a short burst. Pieces flew from the aeroplane and he started smoking, but climbed out of the fight. It was a pilot's dream. I'd never seen such a complete massacre of the enemy in my life. I was afraid someone would wake me up.'

1Lt R J 'Rocky' Byrne flew in the 64th FS/57th FG for more than five months after gaining his first aerial victory before scoring again with three Bf 109 kills during the 'Goose Shoot' of 18 April in P-40K 'White 32'. He rounded out his scoring eight days later by knocking down two more Bf 109s to bring his total to six (*Lou Mastriani*)

Whittaker's four victories brought his total to seven, making him the top-scoring pilot in the 57th FG. It was an honour he would retain throughout the war. At the time, he also stood as the top ace of the Ninth Air Force. Returning to the US in June 1943, Whittaker became a flight instructor for the US Military Academy at West Point and ended the war as a major. He remained in military service, serving later in the Korean War and retiring with the rank of colonel in 1973.

Also scoring for the 65th FS on the mission was 2Lt Alfred Froning, who shot down two Ju 52/3ms and would become an ace in December 1943 while flying P-47s with the squadron.

The 64th FS provided extremely effective top cover for the other squadrons, knocking down a total of six Bf 109s without loss. One of the top-cover pilots was 1Lt R J 'Rocky' Byrne, who 'made ace' a week later. Here is his report, given shortly after landing from the mission;

'The ME's were all messed up. I got three of them, but that isn't

This wrecked Ju 52/3m transport aeroplane was found on Cape Bon by members of the 314th FS/324th FG after the Axis surrender in North Africa. It is almost certainly one of the 60 Junkers tri-motors credited as destroyed to pilots of the 57th FG and the 314th FS on 18 April 1943 (*Andrew D'Antoni*)

Col Art Salisbury, CO of the 57th FG (far right, at the very edge of the photograph), reads a letter of congratulations to his pilots from Gen George C Marshall, chairman of the joint chiefs of staff, following the 18 April 'Goose Shoot' (*via Dan and Melinda Shobe*)

A casually attired 1Lt R J 'Jay' Overcash of the 64th FS/57th FG poses in the cockpit of his P-40K-1 42-46046 'White 13' at Hani Main, in Tunisia, soon after scoring his final two kills to 'make ace' on the afternoon of 26 April 1943.

anything. I had a ringside seat for the whole show. All you could see were those big ships coming apart in the air, plunging into the sea and crashing in flames on the beach. Their fighters couldn't get in to bother our "ball carriers" at all.'

The final victory tally for the mission was as follows – 64th FS downed six Bf 109s and shared in the destruction of a Ju 52/3m; 65th FS downed three Bf 109s, two Bf 110s (although German sources claim there were none of these twin-engined fighters in the area at that time) and 12 Ju 52/3ms; 66th FS downed three Bf 109s and 23$^{1/2}$ Ju 52/3ms; and the 314th FS downed two Bf 109s and 22 Ju 52/3ms. In addition, 324th FG CO Lt Col W K 'Sandy' McNown was credited with two Ju 52/3ms destroyed.

McNown, who had had little opportunity to fly combat missions up to that time, had pencilled himself in as a wingman for Lt Duffy that day because of the high probability of encountering enemy aircraft. He made the most of the opportunity, commenting later that 'I practically burned my guns out'.

The Warhawk pilots had administered a stunning blow to the Luftwaffe, so it was not surprising that the German bombers pounded the field at El Djem on the night of 19 and 20 April in retaliation. Sadly, 1Lt Alan H Smith, a highly decorated 64th FS pilot who had scored 1.5 victories in the 'Goose Shoot', was killed by a bomb fragment, and seven other men were injured. Four P-40s also were destroyed in the raids.

The losses at El Djem, though painful, were inconsequential to the big picture in Tunisia, however. The Warhawk squadrons continued their relentless pounding of the Axis forces on Cape Bon. The 64th FS added the final two names to its list of aces on 26 April, when 2Lts R J 'Rocky' Byrne and R J 'Jay' Overcash destroyed two Bf 109s apiece while escorting RAF Baltimore bombers. The victories brought Byrne's total to six and Overcash's to five.

Both men would soon complete their tours and return home, and they left the service at the end of the war. They were recalled to active duty during the Korean War, and Overcash, who had a career in the textile industry, went on the help design the uniforms for the newly-established Air Force Academy in 1954.

While the 57th FG got the headlines for its 'Goose Shoot', the 79th FG was quietly building a reputation among the bomber

crews of the Ninth Air Force as a top-notch escort outfit. At the same time, the 79th FG was developing its fighter-bomber skills as well. The 316th FS remained attached throughout this period, and several pilots of the newly-arrived 315th FS also flew on 79th FG operations in order to gain experience.

Two similar missions at the end of April stood out. The first took place on the 29th, when 2Lt Richard T Conly of the 315th FS had his first encounter with enemy aircraft, scoring his unit's first confirmed kill. He described it in a letter to his family;

1Lt Richard T Conly scored the first confirmed victory of the 315th FS/324th FG in this P-40F-15 (41-19740) on 29 April 1943 when he shot down a C.202 while escorting P-40s of the 79th FG on a dive-bombing mission. His aeroplane, nicknamed *PING-PANG*, was coded 'White Y55' (*Richard Conly*)

'Our flight was top cover for some other P-40s that were going to bomb some shipping. The first flight had just completed its bombing run when the sky seemed to be full of Me-109s and Macchi 202s. There were suddenly two Macchis diving on us from the rear. I was number two, and happened to see the Macchis first. I called in to Barney Turner (86th FS), my flight leader. We turned into them. I took the first one and Barney took the second. That was the last time I saw my flight.

'The Macchi and I came head-on at each other and I could see his wing guns spurting. It scared me for a second, but then my temper came to my rescue and I was determined to get the bugger. I squeezed the trigger and literally poured lead into him. Suddenly, he started to belch black smoke, rolled over on his back in a split-S and headed down for the deck. I shoved the throttle to the firewall (wide open).

'I chased him from 10,000 ft down to 1000, firing all the time. He was still going straight down and smoking like hell at 1000 ft when I overshot him. I had to pull up and clear my tail, and when I looked again there was a white puddle in the sea. I didn't actually see him go in and neither did the rest, as they were too busy, so I could only claim a probably destroyed on him.

1Lt Wayne Rhynard of the 86th FS/79th FG shakes hands with crew chief S/Sgt Bates Shuping after Rhynard shot down one Bf 109 and damaged a second on 30 April 1943. Rhynard's P-40F-10 (41-19735) was 'White X48', nicknamed *Lucifer's Ghost*. Following the completion of his first combat tour, Rhynard returned to combat flying Mustangs over Europe with the 356th FG (*Wayne Rhynard*)

Flt Off W D Gatling of the 315th FS/ 324th FG walks back to his tent following a practice mission at El Kabrit in April 1943. The practice must have paid off, because on 30 April 1943 Gatling dive-bombed and sank a German destroyer off Cape Bon on just his fourth combat mission (*W D Gatling*)

'When I pulled back up, I had just climbed to about 7000 ft when another '202 jumped me at nine o'clock high. I turned into him, and he started turning to get on my tail. At this point I really swore by a P-40, because I could dogfight and out-turn him with ease. He saw I was going to get a shot and headed for the deck, straight down. I never got farther than 100 yards behind him, and he stayed right in my sights. I watched my tracers pound into him all the way. Those good old six "fifties" raked him from the tail up. He hit the deck about 50 ft just offshore and went straight in. I almost got wet in the splash.'

On the very next day, 30 April, Flt Off W D Gatling of the 315th FS sank a German destroyer off Cape Bon with a 500-lb bomb on just his fourth combat mission. Flying in a 12-aeroplane formation with the 316th FS, Gatling pushed over to attack the ship behind his flight leader and squadron commander, Capt Julian 'Shorty' Adams. Gatling described the experience in his privately-published book, *Critical Points*;

'As you look over the nose of the P-40, you aim through a fixed iron "cross-hair" sight that is located between the cockpit windshield and the propeller. You can feel the aircraft shake a little as you squeeze the gun trigger and fire your six guns. The bomb-release handle – a simple wooden T-handle attached to a metal cable – must be pulled at a co-ordinated time to place the bomb on the target.

'You can tell by the sound of the engine and the propeller that the airspeed is very high and increasing. The gunsight – and the P-40 – starts slowly pulling to the right of the target, and you concentrate more on keeping the gunsight directly on the zig-zagging destroyer. As the airspeed continues to increase, you are having a major problem keeping the gunsight on the target.

'Through all the frustration, confusion and inexperience, you don't think about what is causing this problem. Tracers are coming at you, the airspeed is getting higher, and the altitude is getting lower and lower (below 900 ft at this point). You must do something quick. You give it all you've got! Kick hard left rudder, pull back on the stick and pull the bomb-release handle, all at the same time, trying to toss the bomb to the left.

'You see 500 ft on the altimeter as the nose of the P-40 passes through the horizon on your pullout. Your chin, along with your ears and eyeballs, feel stretched to your belt buckle. As you finish the pull out you almost black out. You look over your shoulder as you gain altitude and see the bomb explode on the mid-deck of the destroyer just forward of the smokestack. You've made a lucky hit!'

Lucky or skilful, Gatling had a long and fruitful combat career in the 324th FG. Before returning to the US as a captain in September 1944, he completed 200 combat missions and logged 300 hours of combat flight time.

The last USAAF aerial victory over North Africa took place on 10 May 1943, when 2Lt George T Lee of the 87th FS/79th FG shot down an Fw 190 fighter-bomber of II./SG 2 over Cape Bon. Two days later, with the vaunted *Afrika Korps* now surrounded and thoroughly beaten, Gen von Arnim surrendered, and the long battle for control of North Africa came to a close. For the Warhawk pilots, however, the war still had a long way to go.

THE NOT-SO-SOFT UNDERBELLY

With North Africa now safely out of Axis hands, Allied leaders immediately began looking across the Mediterranean Sea toward Italy in mid-May 1943. Their first stop on the route through the tragically misnamed 'soft underbelly' of Europe would be Sicily, but first they needed to neutralise the Italian-held island of Pantelleria.

Located halfway between the tip of Cape Bon and the coast of Sicily, Pantelleria was a 42-square-mile rock that bristled with observation posts and aerials for direction-finding radios, not to mention heavy fortifications and a large airfield with underground hangers carved into a rock cliff. The invasion of Sicily, codenamed Operation *Husky*, would be seriously imperilled as long as Pantelleria remained in enemy hands.

Expecting a nasty fight to take the island, the Allies decided to lay on a heavy aerial campaign to soften it up prior to sending troops ashore. For these operations, Warhawk units were brought together under the command of the Northwest African Air Forces (NAAF), along with medium bomber units of both Air Forces. The NAAF assault on

The Italians sheltered their aircraft on Pantelleria (a 42-square-mile rock located halfway between the tip of Cape Bon and the coast of Sicily) in underground hangers such as this one, carved into a rock cliff. After heavy Allied air strikes in May and June 1943, the Italians surrendered the island without a fight (*Bernard Byrne*)

Capt Joseph A Bloomer Jr of the 318th FS/325th FG scored his second victory on 6 June 1943 while flying P-40F-15 (41-19893) 'White 40', nicknamed *Trixie*, over Pantelleria. Note the application of the 325th FG's famous checkertail markings, which began to appear on its Warhawks in June 1943 (*via Dwayne Tabatt*)

1Lt Paul G McArthur of the 87th FS/79th FG shot down four enemy aircraft over Pantelleria on 10 June 1943 before bailing out of his smoking Warhawk. He landed in the sea and was rescued, returning to his unit wet but unhurt the following day. McArthur claimed a fifth confirmed victory on 13 August 1943 to become the 79th FG's only ace of the war (*Paul G McArthur*)

Pantelleria commenced on 18 May 1943, and averaged more than 100 sorties a day through the end of the month. Little or no aerial opposition was met from either Italian fighter units on the island or the German Bf 109 *gruppen* on Sicily.

When the NAAF stepped up the intensity of its attack on 6 June, the Luftwaffe finally responded. On an afternoon dive-bombing mission that day, 23 P-40s of the 325th FG were jumped by an equal number of Bf 109s, and six Warhawk pilots were credited with confirmed victories for no losses. One of the victorious pilots, Capt Joe Bloomer of the 318th FS, described the encounter as 'duck soup'. Pilots of the 57th and 79th FGs submitted claims for two victories each the following day, and the 33rd FG got into the act on the 9th when 1Lt Kenneth B Scidmore of the 60th FS damaged a Bf 109.

The Pantelleria campaign reached its peak on 10 June, when NAAF fighters claimed 34 enemy aeroplanes destroyed, three probables and eight damaged. Nearly half of the day's total fell to the 87th FS/79th FG 'Skeeters' in a single early afternoon mission. Arriving off the north-east corner of the island, the 16 Warhawks were flying at 5000 ft when 1Lt Paul G McArthur spotted a C.202 approaching the top section and he gave chase. McArthur rode up the tail of the Macchi and opened fire, watching his shells hit home before the stricken aeroplane crashed into the sea.

A few moments later, mission leader Lt Col Charles E Grogan saw a large 'hospital' aeroplane flying low over the water, escorted by ten Bf 109s. It was one of the rare opportunities when P-40s in the MTO were presented with a height advantage over the Messerschmitt fighter, and Grogan made the most of it. Leading his flight downward in a diving attack, he knocked down a Bf 109 close to the water, and each member of his flight – Lts Asa Adair, Kensley Miller and Morris Watkins – followed in turn with kills of their own.

Now Capt Frank M Huff spotted a second 'hospital' aeroplane with a similar escort, and he led his flight down in a similar attack. He and Lt Leo Berinati each picked off a Bf 109 close to water. Capt Lee V Gossick's flight went down with Huff's and had even more success – Gossick destroyed one Bf 109 and damaged another, while his wingman, Lt Wyman D Anderson, shot down two C.202s.

Lt McArthur's top cover also joined the show, with 2Lt John Kirsch diving from 5000 ft to knock down a Bf 109, while McArthur destroyed a second C.202 and two Bf 109s, as well as damaging a third Messerschmitt fighter. That brought the victory tally for the mission to 15 destroyed. The fight took a toll on McArthur's P-40F, however, and his engine began to smoke either due to over-exertion by the pilot or a hit from an enemy fighter.

The young pilot bailed out into the sea about 30 miles off the coast of Tunisia and he climbed into his half-inflated dinghy while several Warhawks circled overhead to help direct an air-sea rescue aeroplane to him. Just before dark, an RAF Walrus flying boat arrived on the scene and landed to pick up Lt McArthur. He clambered aboard the rescue aircraft, and its pilot turned into the wind to take off, but the now heavily-laden biplane declined to co-operate. It bumped along the water, but stubbornly refused to lift off.

Finally, the pilot decided to taxi the Walrus toward land, but soon thereafter the engine quit. McArthur helped man the bilge pumps as the aeroplane bobbed in the Mediterranean through the night. Early the next morning a British destroyer arrived on the scene and towed the aeroplane back to port. A soggy McArthur returned to his unit on 11 June, while a British assault force headed for the beaches of Pantelleria. When the invaders arrived, the Italians promptly surrendered the island.

An interesting sidelight to the Pantelleria campaign was the combat debut of the 99th FS. This unit, consisting entirely of black personnel, was assigned to the 33rd FG, and flew its first mission on 2 June when it strafed Italian positions on Pantelleria. Equipped with P-40Ls, the 99th FS was commanded by Maj Benjamin O Davis Jr, who was a West Point graduate and the son of a US Army general.

The pilots of the 99th FS, flying first as wingmen in 33rd FG formations and later on their own, averaged two missions a day over Pantelleria. They quickly became accustomed to the strafing, dive-bombing and bomber-escort operations, but their only clash with enemy aircraft, on 9 June, produced no aerial victories or losses. The squadron stood down for a week after the end of the Pantelleria campaign, but on 2 July the 99th FS notched its first aerial victory when 1Lt Charles B Hall shot down an Fw 190 over Sicily while escorting B-25s to Castelvetrano.

The invasion of Sicily was now less than a week away.

'CHECKERTAILS' OVER SARDINIA

While most of the NAAF's attention was focused on Pantelleria following the victory in North Africa, other targets beckoned as well. For the 325th FG, which in June began painting the tail surfaces of its P-40s with distinctive black and yellow checkers, the summer of 1943 would be dominated by a series of missions across the Mediterranean to Sardinia. The purpose of these missions was to keep the defending Axis fighters occupied so they would not be available to assist in the defence of Sicily.

1Lt Herschel H Green of the 317th FS/325th FG barely survived his first encounter with German fighters over Sardinia, but nevertheless went on to become the top ace of the 'Checkertails'. He is shown here with his groundcrew and replacement P-40F-5 41-14512 in the late summer of 1943 at Mateur. 'Herky' Green's 18 confirmed victories in P-40s, P-47s and P-51s made him the second-highest scoring USAAF ace in the MTO (*Herschel Green photo via Dwayne Tabatt*)

It was during the 325th FG's campaign over Sardinia that the 'Checkertails' established a reputation for prowess in air-to-air combat that survives to this day. Between mid May and late September, Warhawk pilots of the 325th FG racked up no fewer than 102 victories in 37 missions for the loss of just 16 aeroplanes. In the process, all four of the pilots who would become aces in P-40s scored their fifth victories over Sardinia, and several future aces opened their scoring tallies on these missions.

The 325th FG flew its first mission to Cagliari, Sardinia, on 13 May. Thirty-four Warhawks escorted bombers northward from the Tunisian coast across 100 miles of sea to the target and back without interference. From this uneventful start, the campaign quickly grew to full fury six days later, when 32 Warhawks escorted B-26s to Decimomannu airfield, where the bombers were to attack a supply depot. Eleven aggressive Bf 109s jumped the escort fighters from above, and soon a big dogfight was under way.

Two future aces of the 325th FG scored their first successes among the five victories confirmed on 19 May. Maj Bob Baseler of group headquarters and 1Lt Herschel H 'Herky' Green of the 317th FS, who was on his first combat mission, got one apiece. Green only recalled firing a long burst at some passing Bf 109s early in the fight before two Luftwaffe pilots singled him out. Flying his P-40 like a combat veteran rather than the rookie he was, Green knew his P-40 could not climb above the Bf 109s or run away from them in level flight. His only choice was to turn into their attacks, and turn he did.

Soon the Luftwaffe pilots began co-ordinating their attacks so that if Green turned into one of them, the other would be on his tail. The P-40 took numerous hits, including one 20 mm blast in the fuselage that knocked out Green's radio and thudded against the armour plate behind his seat. With his panic rising, the American flipped the Warhawk into an over-the-top snap roll. The aeroplane stalled, then fell into a power-on spin. It was still spinning when Green reached a layer of clouds and then recovered. Shaken but unhurt, he nursed the Warhawk back across the sea to his base at Montesquieu, in Tunisia. Following his landing, Green's aeroplane was hauled off to the junkyard.

But the future ace learned that his squadron commander, Capt Bill Reed, had seen a Bf 109 go down after Green had fired at it. This marked the first of 18 victories Green would score while flying P-40s, P-47s and P-51s in the 325th FG. He finished the war as the second-highest scoring USAAF ace in the MTO.

Not satisfied with the results of the bombing on 19 May, the NAAF ordered a similar mission to Decimomannu the next day. On

Maj Robert L Baseler of the 325th FG headquarters opened his scoring on 19 May 1943 when he shot down a Bf 109 over Sardinia. Seen here with USO stars Frances Langford and Bob Hope, Baseler named his P-40F-20 41-20006 *STUD*. The aeroplane's crew chief, taking advantage of Baseler's keen sense of humour, added the name *MORTIMER SNERD* (a popular cartoon character of the day) on the cowling (*Robert Baseler photo via Dwayne Tabatt*)

Belva, alias P-40L-1 42-10476 'White 89', was the personal aircraft of Flt Off John W Smallsreed of the 319th FS/325th FG. After scoring three victories over Sardinia between 19 and 27 May, he was posted missing in action on 28 May 1943 (*via Dwayne Tabatt*)

this strike the bombing was much more successful, and the 325th FG shot down six more defending fighters over the target. One of them fell to 1Lt Frank J 'Spot' Collins, the second of five victories he would score in Warhawks. Then, while returning from the mission, a flight of P-40s led by the group commander, Lt Col Gordon H Austin, spotted seven Me 323 Gigante transports flying at low altitude across the sea. The huge aeroplanes stood no chance, and the Warhawk pilots systematically shot them all down into the sea.

2Lt George P Novotny was serving as a replacement pilot with the 317th FS/325th FG when he scored three times over Sardinia during July and August 1943. He went on to claim five more victories after the group transitioned to P-47s. Although Novotny is shown here with Warhawk 'White 14', he did not have a personal aircraft assigned to him until later in his combat tour (*George Novotny*)

This often-published photo shows Capt Ralph G 'Zack' Taylor Jr's P-40L-1 (42-10436) 'White 13' *Duchess of Durham IV* after Taylor had scored his fourth, fifth and sixth victories on 20 July 1943. What it does not show is the name *My Gal Sal* which was painted on the right side of the aeroplane's nose. Taylor is kneeling, second from the left (*Hartman Leite photo via Dwayne Tabatt*)

Now the 325th FG was rolling, and in six more missions to Sardinia through to the end of June its pilots scored 23 victories. The group spent the first three weeks of July concentrating on supporting the Sicilian invasion. Then, on 20 July, the 'Checkertails' went back to Sardinia and came home to toast their first ace. Capt Ralph G 'Zack' Taylor shot down

Maj Bob Baseler, one of four 325th FG P-40 aces, made extensive modifications to his Warhawk, removing two guns and other equipment to lighten it in the hope of improving its high-altitude performance. After *STUD* was retired from combat operations, it was repainted in a striking colour scheme of overall gloss black with red trim, and used as a group hack (*Andrew Musgrave photo via Dwayne Tabatt*)

two Bf 109s and an C.202 to bring his score to six confirmed, a total that was never topped while the group was equipped with P-40s. Also scoring that day was a young replacement pilot in the 317th FS, 2Lt George P Novotny, who recalled the mission 57 years later;

'I believe our squadron put up 12 or 16 P-40s on our second mission that day. We were to frag bomb and strafe the airfield at Cagliari, Sardinia. We flew on the deck – 50 to 100 ft – across the Mediterranean to the harbour at Cagliari, then right across the city to the airfield, which was very close to the city. As we approached there were a number of enemy fighters taking off. Some were circling. My estimate was about eight to ten aeroplanes.

'We got into a large circle of aeroplanes. Some C.202s were going around the circle the opposite way, head-on with us. I nearly collided with one of them. I could see the flashes from his guns, and I fired as he passed me. There was a trail of smoke and fire coming from his engine. As I came around in a circle, I could see that the '202 was trying to put down next to a road. He bellied in. I could not see if the pilot got out, as there was a lot of smoke and fire, and the aeroplane skidded and broke up. Flt Off Donovan confirmed what I saw.'

Novotny went on to score eight victories in the 325th FG before completing his combat tour in June 1944. Because of his junior status in the 317th FS during the summer of 1943, he was not assigned a regular aircraft until after the unit had traded its P-40s for P-47s.

1Lt Walter B 'Bud' Walker (centre) of the 317th FS/325th FG scored his third, fourth and fifth victories on 30 July 1943 over Sardinia in his P-40F-15 (41-19896) 'White 25'. Posing with the groundcrewman at right is the squadron's canine mascot (*Ira Grandel photo via Dwayne Tabatt*)

More big days followed over Sardinia. Maj Bob Baseler got two of the 325th FG's 17 victories on 22 July, and then on 26 July he claimed one more to bring his total to five, thus making him the second 'Checkertail' ace. The 319th FS suffered a sad loss on 28 July when its CO, Capt Everett B Howe, was shot down by flak, but the group bounced back two days later to enjoy its most successful day of the campaign.

The mission on 30 July was a routine sweep over southern Sardinia by 32 P-40s of the 317th and 319th FSs. They were initially jumped by 25-30 Bf 109s, and then a second force of Messerschmitt fighters and C.202s piled in. During the ensuing dogfight, the Americans claimed 21 victories for the loss of just one P-40. In the post-mission reports, the Warhawk pilots noted that the enemy fighters tried to turn with them, rather than using the normal 'dive-and-zoom' tactics, which may account for the unusually high number of claims.

A German researcher has studied this encounter closely, and believes the fighters were from III./JG 77. That unit's records show only five losses for the day, but on the other hand its pilots claimed five victories although only one P-40 went down. As might be expected in a wide-spread engagement that involved dozens of twisting and turning aircraft, overclaiming of kills seems to have taken place on both sides.

Be that as it may, the 325th FG was awarded a Distinguished Unit Citation for the mission, and also added another name to its list of aces

Capt John C A Watkins of 325th FG headquarters poses with his crew chief, Sgt Misenheimer, and their P-40L-5 (42-10866) 'White 59' *Big Helen III* in September 1943. Watkins is credited with gaining permission for the 325th FG to apply the checkerboard marking on the tails of its aircraft (*via Dwayne Tabatt*)

that day. 1Lt Walter B 'Bud' Walker of the 317th FS was credited with three kills, bringing his total to five. During the fight, Walker found himself taking on three Bf 109s alone. He shot down two of the attackers as the fight circled lower and lower, but by then the third Bf 109 was firmly on his tail and pounding Walker's P-40 with cannon fire. Flying just above the trees, the American hauled his Warhawk into a tight turn – the Bf 109 pilot tried to follow, but his less manoeuvrable fighter snap-rolled and crashed into the ground.

The 325th FG's final claims over Sardinia – and its final claims in P-40s – came on 28 August during a dive-bombing mission against a factory at Fluminimaggoire. As was so often the case, the Warhawks were jumped from above and behind, but were able to turn the tables on their attackers. Jettisoning their bombs and turning into the attack, the top-cover P-40 pilots claimed seven destroyed, with just two of their own damaged. Capt Frank J 'Spot' Collins was credited with one Bf 109 shot down, increasing his tally to five, and making him the last Warhawk ace of the 325th FG.

The 'Checkertails' flew six more missions to Sardinia, capping off the campaign with an uneventful sweep over the island on 14 September. A week later the island surrendered, and two days after that the 325th FG stood down to begin its transition to a new fighter – the massive Republic P-47 Thunderbolt. The group's Warhawks were spread among the four remaining P-40 groups in the MTO, their colourful chequered tails being painted out with a drab coat of camouflage.

THE INVASION OF SICILY

While the aerial campaigns against Pantelleria and Sardinia were spectacular and successful, the Allies' invasion of Sicily was the high point of the war in the MTO during the summer of 1943. The NAAF threw its full force into the process of softening up Sicily, starting as soon as Pantelleria fell. Massive formations of medium and heavy bombers, covered by swarms of fighters, ranged over Sicily beginning in late June, attacking airfields, lines of transportation and communications, supply depots and anything else they could find of military value. Axis fighter units on the island responded as best they could, but they were greatly outnumbered and doomed to failure.

Of the NAAF P-40 units involved in the pre-invasion operations over Sicily, the 324th FG, operating as an independent unit for the first time, and with the 99th FS attached, saw the most action. The group's three squadrons – the 314th, 315th and 316th FSs – had reunited on 18 June at El Houaria, on Cape Bon. After a week of flying defensive patrols over Pantelleria, the group was ordered out on a fighter sweep over southern Sicily on 1 July. For two weeks after that, such missions became a daily chore for the 324th FG pilots. One of those pilots was 1Lt Sidney W Brewer of the 315th FS, who recounted his experience in a privately published memoir;

'The pre-invasion campaign to Sicily was undoubtedly the most dangerous of all my combat flying. It involved a long (150 miles) overwater flight, which gave the Germans plenty of time to prepare a proper reception for us, and they did. We flew 72-ship formations, and we had

Maj Fred Delany, right, and Capt Bob Dempsey were CO and operations officer respectively of the 316th FS/ 324th FG. They are seen posing with Delany's P-40F at Causeway LG in March 1943. The aeroplane (probably 'White Y70'), carries the 316th FS 'Hell's Belles' badge plus the personal name *PETITE I*. Delany was shot down and badly wounded in this aeroplane on one of the squadron's first missions, and Dempsey assumed command – he was killed in action over Sicily in July 1943 (*Ron Elling*)

THE NOT-SO-SOFT UNDERBELLY

73

some success with it, but they too had success. By and large, we suffered more losses than they did.

'Frequently, 100-plus German fighters would intercept us, and grand air battles were almost a daily event. We soon wore them down, however, and their attacks on us were less and less effective in ever decreasing numbers. By 10 July, when our ground forces landed in Sicily, we had obtained complete mastery of the air. The period 1 through to 16 July proved to be the most crucial of all my experiences to that time. I flew 12 missions to Sicily during that time – many involved night take-off so as to be there at first light. Our losses were heavy. For example, on 8 July we lost ten pilots and as many aeroplanes, including *Brittle II*, which was my aeroplane. She went into the ocean after one of our guys bailed out of her. Later that day I got a new aeroplane, and it was destroyed when I had to belly it in upon returning from a mission. It was a hard two weeks, and we were all tired and combat-weary by the end of it.'

The 324th FG had a tough time over Sicily, losing nine pilots in two weeks, including the 316th FS CO, Maj Bob Dempsey. But the group also inflicted its share of damage on the Axis defenders, destroying 21 enemy fighters between 2 and 10 July.

Several of the group's pilots, including Capt Bruce Hunt and 1Lt Andrew D'Antoni of the 314th FS, and 1Lt Charles Harrington of the 316th FS, were awarded Distinguished Flying Crosses for individual acts of bravery during the period. In addition, the pilot who would become the 324th FG's last ace scored his first pair of victories on 9 July. 1Lt James E 'Murph' Fenex was leading a flight of 316th FS Warhawks on an escort mission to Castel Vetrano LG when the formation came under attack. Flying with Fenex that day was 1Lt James T Johnson, who wrote this account;

'I was flying "Murph's" wing, and (1Lt William H) Snyder and (1Lt Emile J) Selig made up the second element. Ours was the sandwich flight of the 12-ship mission. Our Spitfire top cover was engaged about the time we crossed the Sicilian coastline. As the B-25s turned left to set up the bomb run, our top flight was attacked by two Me-109s, and immediately

After the 325th FG converted to P-47s in September 1943, its P-40s were transferred to other units within the Twelfth Air Force. One such example was Zack Taylor's *Duchess of Durham IV*, which is seen here in service with the 314th FS/ 324th FG as the personal mount of Capt Bruce E Hunt. Note how the checkertail has been painted out and the aeroplane's serial number reapplied. The name and pin-up girl painting on the nose were carry-overs from Taylor, but the white lip on the radiator scoop is new, possibly identifying 'White 11' as a flight leader's aircraft (*Bruce Hunt*)

1Lt J T Johnson of the 316th FS/ 324th FG saw extensive action over Sicily, scoring a confirmed victory on 9 July 1943 in a wild skirmish after losing his flight leader, future ace 1Lt James E Fenex. Johnson flew two combat tours in the 316th FS, finishing the war as squadron CO with 200 missions to his credit (*Troy Upton photo via Bill McCool*)

two more came at us from behind and to our right.

'Fenex called, "Duck right!" These two had a more shallow angle of attack than usual. As we were in the turn, it was obvious that "Murph" would be able to get his man with a head-on attack before he could get out of range, and Snyder seemed to be in position to attack number two. At a time like that your head is on a swivel – it has to be. Over my left shoulder I saw (more fighters), and I realised that I would have to leave my element leader. They were coming in steeper than usual, above the bombers, but with us as their targets.

'I said, "Gotta break left, 'Murph'", and pulled a tight chandelle left. The first '109 had already started his pull-up but seemed to be firing. The second one continued his steep dive. I was losing airspeed fast, but I felt sure he'd be in range before I stalled. I hosed a long, out-of-range burst for effect, and he started to pull out of the dive, to try to avoid a head-on pass, I guess. But he was too steep and mushed into my range.

'I had to roll left nearly onto my back and pull Gs so hard I almost blacked out. I relaxed the stick at the point I thought he would be, and I guessed right. He was right there in my gunsight. I started firing and pulled in a little more lead. The first burst cut his fuselage in two where the cross was painted on.

'I didn't have even one second to gloat. Before I could start to look around, there was a terrific explosion and my canopy glass shattered, the frame and all disappearing. My immediate reaction was hard left forward stick and hard right rudder. If there is a word speedier than immediate, that would be a better word to describe my reaction. That manoeuvre had to be the nearest thing to an outside snap roll that a P-40 will do. I was alive, but still in deep trouble.

'On recovery, I found myself headed north with no canopy, an engine overheat light on and still alone. I had not seen or even suspected the SOB that shot me, and now I couldn't even find an enemy, much less a friend. I did a diving 180-degree turn, came out of boost and eased the throttle back to cruise setting. I set a course to the nearest water south, expecting to be having Me-109 company at any time. It became necessary to level off and slow down a little bit because the wind was about to beat me to death. I cleared Sicily and continued down to 2000 ft, where I got some comfort from the fact that my overheat light had gone out. It was still a long way to Cape Bon, so I held 2000 ft while I tried to make myself decide whether it would be better to bail out or ditch in the water if the engine should quit.

'The mission debriefing was still going on, and I was being reported missing, when I dragged my wounded P-40 in on a straight-in approach. I didn't have any idea how bad things looked until I saw the groundcrews' faces turn white. Someone helped me out of the cockpit and showed me the big hole and peeled-back aluminium behind the cockpit armour plate where an explosive 20 mm or two had hit. My face and hands were scratched and bloody with minor cuts from flying glass when the canopy shattered, but I must have looked like a walking-around cadaver. I was mighty glad to be back, but it couldn't have created more stir if a real ghost had walked into Ops. It was still a grim time – Selig didn't make it back.'

The next day, the pilots at El Houaria were awakened long before daylight to prepare for the mission they had been anticipating for two weeks. They were ordered off at 0425 hrs to provide cover for the landings on Sicily. The big show was on, and the 324th FG would be in the thick of it. One pilot who remembered it vividly was Capt Lester L Krause Jr of the 314th FS;

Early on the morning of 10 July 1943, Capt Lester Krause of the 314th FS/324th FG led the first patrol of P-40s over the landing beaches on Sicily. Flying Warhawk 'White Y14', Krause dodged 'friendly' flak from the invasion fleet before spotting a Ju 88 and shooting it down. Krause eventually commanded both the 314th and 315th FSs, reaching the rank of lieutenant colonel by the end of the war (*Les Krause*)

'I was the leader of the first fighter cover to arrive before daybreak to protect the invasion fleet off the coast at Licata. We had communications procedures to advise the Command Centre of the fleet when we were in position. When we were approaching the fleet, I reported in and received an acknowledgement. However, that didn't stop the fleet from firing at us. I moved the formation out of range. I communicated with them again and received the reply that they would hold their fire. We moved in and got fired at again. This continued to happen, so we finally just stayed out of their range.

'It was during one of these staying-out-of-range episodes that I caught a glimpse of an aeroplane. It was still dark, but as I closed on the aircraft I identified it as a Ju-88. It must have been specially equipped for night flying, as I couldn't see any exhaust flame. When I fired there was no explosion or fire. I must have hit the crew and they lost control. It spiralled down and crashed into the sea. I don't think it was part of a bombing formation. I think it was a recce keeping an eye on the fleet.'

Capt Krause's claim was the last of the campaign for the 324th FG. The group flew a series of escort missions for C-47s en route to Sicily until the end of July, and then it moved back to Causeway LG, Tunisia, where it would remain inactive until October.

While the 324th FG was flying its missions from Cape Bon to Sicily, the 33rd FG was performing similar duties from its newly-captured base on Pantelleria. The 57th and 79th FGs were not employed until after the landings. Once the Allied ground forces began to advance on Sicily, the Luftwaffe fighter units were forced to withdraw to landing grounds near

Foggia, in Italy. The rest of the campaign involved primarily fighter-bomber work, although two more P-40 pilots reached ace status during this period.

The first was Maj John Bradley, CO of the 58th FS/33rd FG. On 12 July, while leading a patrol over the Licata invasion beaches, Bradley saw a flight in his formation get jumped from above by two flights of Bf 109s that set up a criss-cross pattern of dive-and-zoom attacks.

One P-40 was shot down in the initial attack, while 2Lt Jack Skipper turned into the oncoming Bf 109s and shot one down in a head-on pass. Then Bradley led his flight into the melee and spotted a Messerschmitt on the tail of a P-40. Bradley turned to get behind the Bf 109, and it began to climb. He fired a long burst into the belly of the enemy aeroplane and saw pieces fly off before it turned over and dived into the sea. Bradley, now an ace with five victories, completed his combat tour soon thereafter, and returned to the US, leaving the service at the end of the war. He was recalled to the USAF in 1951 to fly P-51 fighter-bombers in Korea.

A month after the Licata landings, Allied troops were approaching the key port city of Messina, and the struggle for Sicily was nearing its end. On 13 August, 12 P-40s of the 87th FS/79th FG (carrying 500-lb bombs) were assigned to fly an anti-shipping patrol over the Straits of Messina with four RAF Spitfires providing top cover.

The P-40s found a large transport ship two miles off Bagnara and attacked it, scoring one hit on the stern and two near misses. After the bomb run, the P-40s were attacked from above at 10,000 ft by ten-plus Bf 109s and Fw 190s. 1Lt Paul G McArthur, flying P-40L 'White X99', managed to get behind one of the Bf 109s and hit it with a telling burst of fire. The German fighter went down in flames, and McArthur's wingman, 1Lt Leo Berinati, saw it crash into the sea. One P-40 was shot down in the scrap before the German fighters withdrew.

Later, the formation was attacked again, and McArthur returned Berinati's favour by confirming a Bf 109 shot down by his wingman. McArthur's victory, his fifth and last, gave him the unique distinction of being the 79th FG's only ace of the war. He flew combat again in the Korean conflict, this time at the controls of B-29 heavy bombers, and after retiring from the USAF, pursued a law career in his native Alabama.

During the same fight on 13 August, 1Lt Morris H Watkins scored an unusual victory without firing a shot. While attacking a Messerschmitt, he was in turn set upon by three others and hit in the right arm. He reached over to the control stick with his left hand and pulled the trigger, then watched as tracers ripped into the Bf 109 in front of him. The German fighter crashed into the sea and Watkins – not badly wounded – returned to base to claim the aircraft destroyed.

Sgt Rocco Loscalzo, a crew chief in the 87th FS/79th FG, works on P-40L 'White X99', which was the aircraft in which 1Lt Paul G McArthur scored his fifth victory on 13 August 1943 to become the 79th FG's only ace. Note how the white bars have been added to the national insignia by painting over the squadron number – a common practice in the 79th FG (*Rocco Loscalzo*)

The crew chief pauses from his work on P-40L-20 42-11094 *LITTLE DUGE II* in Sicily during the late summer of 1943. The aeroplane's regular pilot was Maj Charles Duncan, CO of the 59th FS/33rd FG. His four confirmed victories are displayed as diving silhouettes of one Bf 109 and three C.202s behind the name on the cowling. The white tail stripe is a squadron identification marking (*Dr John Woodworth photo via George Dively Jr*)

He was surprised when the armourer of his aeroplane informed him that the P-40s guns had not been fired, so he withdrew his claim. However, further investigation revealed that gunfire from the Bf 109s attacking Watkins had hit the Bf 109 in front of him, and the P-40 pilot was given credit for the kill.

STALEMATE IN ITALY

The NAAF had already begun its softening-up aerial campaign against mainland Italy when the remaining Axis forces on Sicily surrendered on 17 August 1943. By this time, three P-40 groups – the 33rd, 57th and 79th FGs – were operating from Sicilian airfields, while the 324th FG remained inactive in Tunisia and the 325th FG completed its campaign against Sardinia prior to giving up its P-40s. Meanwhile, the Ninth Air Force had departed for England to become the tactical air component of the cross-channel invasion force, and its three P-40 groups had duly shifted commands to the Twelfth Air Force.

The British 8th Army commenced the invasion of Italy on 3 September with landings on the 'toe' of the nation's 'boot' at Reggio di Calabria. Just five days later the Italian government capitulated, having deposed dictator Mussolini in late July. Now with German forces as their only foe, the Allies staged two more landings, at Taranto and Salerno, on 9 September. The three P-40 groups on Sicily provided support for the invasion forces by

1Lt Paul L Carll of the 64th FS/57th FG flies Warhawk 'White 32' over Scordia, Sicily, on 16 September 1943 – just two days before the group moved to mainland Italy. This P-40L-1 (42-10453) displays the 64th FS 'Black Scorpions' badge, along with a red flash extending around the nose. It also carries six wing guns, and its serial is painted near the top of the tail above the RAF fin flash (*Bruce Abercrombie*)

flying patrols and escorting medium bombers attacking German lines of communication.

Up to this point, Warhawks pilots had found little air opposition over Italy. A flight of P-40Ls from the 59th FS/33rd FG scored first over the mainland, claiming three Bf 109s destroyed and two probables near Lamezia on 26 August. The next encounter came on 3 September, when 2Lt Paul L Carll of the 64th FS/57th FG shot down a Bf 109 over Catanzaro and 2Lt Eugene Kowalski of the same unit damaged another.

The Salerno invasion, codenamed Operation *Avalanche*, did not go well during the first few days, but by 13 September the ground forces had secured the airfield at Montecorvino, and the Warhawks of the 33rd FG moved in immediately. The group's pilots found themselves in the thick of the fighting, with their primary objective being to defend the Salerno beachhead from raiding Luftwaffe fighter-bombers. Salerno was also tough on the groundcrews of the 33rd, as the unit's unofficial history, *Combat Digest*, described;

'The landing was rough, and it took plenty of hard work and guts unloading equipment while Ju-88s gave the beaches a thorough going over. The first few days were hectic. The enemy was in artillery range, and the warships offshore were shelling the hills back into the north of the field. The German breakthrough, a gas scare, plus the air raids and dust made things very uncomfortable.

'The German Air Force was very much alive again, and usually made three raids per day at breakfast, lunch and dinner, plus the night raids. They would come in from the sea, dive-bomb the shipping and pass over the field on the way home, sometimes firing but in too big of a hurry to do much damage. The group's patrols would jump the Jerries as soon as they came off the bomb run and through the terrific barrage of flak from

2Lt Robert B 'Bruce' Abercrombie of the 64th FS/33rd FG christened his P-40F 'White 33' *Ginger*, and the fighter is seen between sorties at Rocco Bernardo, in Italy, in the Autumn of 1943. Loaded with six 40-lb bombs and a full drop tank, it's ready for a mission. Note how a dummy fourth gun port has been painted on the wing, and the hubcaps have also been decorated. When the 57th FG converted to P-47s in December 1943, *Ginger* went to the 315th FS/324th FG, where Lt Dave Giltner flew it as 'White 49' *Marge/Judy* (*Bruce Abercrombie*)

our ship and shore batteries. After about five days of suffering heavy losses, the Jerry raids slowed down and finally ceased altogether, except for the night raids.'

The 33rd FG pilots, highly experienced and spoiling for a good scrape, acquitted themselves well over Salerno. In three days – 15-17 September – they were credited with destroying 14 Bf 109s and Fw 190s for the loss of just one P-40. The scoring was spread among all three squadrons of the group, and the top scorer was 2Lt Morgan S Tyler of the 59th FS with two victories.

The 57th and 79th FGs took up station on the Italian mainland on 15 September. Both groups were assigned to support the British invasion force pushing north from Taranto, and in short order they found themselves moving to bases on the Foggia Plain that had only recently been evacuated by the Luftwaffe.

At this point, the Allied advance in southern Italy ground to a halt. Field Marshal Albert Kesselring, commander of the German forces, had used the rugged terrain to his advantage by managing to establish a defensive barrier across the Italian peninsula roughly 80 miles south of Rome. Called the 'Gustav Line', it stretched from just north of Naples on

99th FS P-40L-1 42-10499 probably came to grief at Capodichino while the squadron was attached to the 79th FG for operations. 'White A10' still carries the markings of its former owners, the 58th FS/33rd FG, specifically the American flag, red tail stripe and yellow wing bands. The dark rectangle on the cowling contains the words *Africa Special* (*George Trittipo*)

Mechanics from the 59th FS/33rd FG tear into a P-40L at Paestum, in Italy, making the most of the sunny autumnal weather during October 1943 (*Bernard Byrne*)

the west coast to the Trigno River in the east. Warhawk pilots would spend the rest of their tenure in the MTO aiding the bloody effort to break through the 'Gustav Line'.

The remaining P-40 units of the Twelfth Air Force moved to Italy in late October. The 324th FG made its new home at Cercola LG, at the foot of Mt Vesuvius near Naples, and the 99th FS joined the 79th FG at Foggia No 3 LG. The 99th FS, now under the command of Maj George S 'Spanky' Roberts, was anxious to get back into action, and with good reason.

The squadron's effectiveness, and the suitability of black pilots in general for combat operations, had been called into question in an unflattering report sent to Washington from the 33rd FG, its original host unit, and signed by Col William W Momyer. While the squadron was preparing to take its P-40s back into combat at Foggia, its former commander, Maj Benjamin O Davis, was in Washington DC fighting a political battle for the squadron's survival.

With the stalemate developing on the ground, and the Luftwaffe now operating from bases north of Rome, Warhawk squadrons in Italy once more found themselves operating as long-range artillery in the fighter-bomber mode, with little opportunity for air-to-air combat.

The experience of the 314th FS/324th FG was typical. From the date of its first mission out of Cercola, 20 October, through the end of the 1943 the 314th FS flew 64 missions, and on every one of them the Warhawks were loaded with 500- or 1000-lb bombs. Following the 33rd FG's flurry of air combat over the Salerno beachhead, P-40 pilots in Italy scored just 15 more victories before the end of the year. Now, German flak and the nasty Italian winter weather were the pilots' most fearsome enemies.

The American invasion at Anzio on 22 January 1944, designed to break the stalemate on the 'Gustav line', provided one last flurry of aerial

Armourers of the 315th FS/324th FG note a squadron milestone at Cercola, in Italy, in December 1943 (*Dick Conly*)

combat for the Warhawk pilots of the Twelfth Air Force. In the process, the 99th FS would finally get the chance to permanently silence its numerous critics.

Allied intelligence estimated that the Luftwaffe had about 300 fighters within striking distance of Anzio, which is on the west coast of Italy about 25 miles south of Rome, so plans were made to establish a constant umbrella of fighters over the invasion beach to provide air defence. Spitfires would provide high cover, while Warhawks of the 33rd, 79th and 324th FGs would patrol below 12,000 ft.

Spitfires drove off the opening attack by bomb-carrying Fw 190s at first light on D-Day. Then at midday the Warhawks got into the action when 16 P-40Ls of the 87th FS/79th FG took on a gaggle of Fw 190s and Bf 109s just north of Anzio, knocking down six while losing one of their own. Similar engagements continued for a week, and by the end of January Warhawk pilots from the three groups had claimed 45 victories over Anzio.

The 99th FS got its long-awaited chance to show its stuff on 27 January 1944. Maj Roberts was leading 15 P-40s on the early morning patrol when they caught 16 Fw 190s pulling out from their bomb run over Anzio harbour. In the sharp engagement that followed,

The 'Tuskegee Airmen' of the 99th FS flew their first combat missions in June 1943, but it was not until the Anzio landings in January 1944 that the black pilots began to run up a score of aerial victories. On 27 January 1944, 1Lt Robert W Deiz shot down an Fw 190 in this particular P-40L-15 (42-10855, 'White A33'). His victory was one of eight credited to 99th FS pilots that day (*Griff Murphy photo via Tom Ivie*)

As the number of Merlin-powered P-40s dwindled in late 1943, the Twelfth Air Force relied on repair and maintenance facilities to keep its Warhawk units supplied with aircraft. This ex-58th FS/33rd FG P-40L-5 (42-10533) had just been rebuilt by Overhaul Depot No 3 at Capodichino, near Naples, and is seen on 8 December 1943 awaiting a fresh paint job, before returning to operations (*Burke photo via J Crow*)

the black pilots claimed five victories, one probable and four damaged. Not a single P-40 went down in the fight. The 99th FS was not finished for the day, however.

On an afternoon mission the squadron again tangled with German fighter-bombers, claiming three destroyed and one probable, but losing one P-40 to the Luftwaffe and one to flak. Then on the following day the 99th scored four more victories. By the end of February, when the aerial threat to Anzio had finally subsided, the 99th FS emerged as the top-scoring P-40 unit over the beachhead with 16 victories. Any doubts about black pilots' combat abilities were now silenced, and the 99th FS would go on to compile a fine record while flying escort missions in P-51s as part of the all-black 332nd FG.

By the spring of 1944, time was catching up with the old P-40. The last Merlin-powered Warhawk, P-40L-20 42-11129, had rolled off the Curtiss assembly in April 1943, and the USAAF did not consider the Allison-powered P-40N suitable for combat against the Luftwaffe. And production of the big Republic P-47, which showed potential as a superlative fighter-bomber, was now in high gear.

314th FS/324th FG Warhawk 'White 13' rests uneasily at Cercola as Mount Vesuvius spews tonnes of ash into the air in March 1944. The group had to evacuate its P-40s to Capodichino on 22 March when falling ash from the eruption threatened the airfield (*Bruce Hunt*)

Capt James E 'Murph' Fenex Jr of the 316th FS/324th FG poses with a captured German flag soon after the end of the African campaign. He was the last P-40 pilot in the MTO to reach ace status, destroying two Fw 190s south of Rome on 29 March 1944 to bring his total to five destroyed, one probable and two damaged. One of the original pilots in the 316th FS, Fenex flew more than 100 missions before returning to the US in April 1944. His regular aircraft was 'White 96', but no photographs of it are known to exist (*Troy Upton photo via Bill McCool*)

In mid-December 1943, the 57th FG followed the path of the 'Checkertails' and transitioned to the Thunderbolt. The 79th FG would also swap types in March 1944. With the 33rd FG transferring to China in the same month, only the 324th FG, with the 99th FS now attached, would remain as a Warhawk outfit.

There was still time for one more pilot to join the ranks of MTO P-40 aces, however. Capt James E Fenex Jr, a flight leader in the 316th FS/324th FG, knocked down an Fw 190 near Anzio on 16 February to bring his total to three confirmed. One of the original pilots in the squadron, 'Murph' Fenex had passed the 100-mission mark, and was known in the squadron for his fearless attitude in combat, taking a special delight in low-level strafing.

On 29 March, just two weeks before he was due to return to the US, Capt Fenex led a mission out of Cercola to the Anzio area, where the Warhawks were assigned to dive-bomb a German supply dump beyond the beachhead. The bombing was successful, starting four large fires, and

Top right
Sgt William Holenchak of the 316th FS/324th FG takes a break after preparing his P-40F-15 (41-19893) *"ANNE"* for its next mission in the early summer of 1944. The aeroplane – probably 'White 84' – has a 1000-lb bomb attached to its belly shackles, plus six small wing bombs. Its original pilot was Capt Joe Bloomer, CO of the 318th FS/325th FG, who called the fighter *Trixie*. The Warhawk displays no fewer than 110 mission markers, as well as the white diamond insignia of the 316th FS. The veteran P-40 survived the war and was condemned to salvage in June 1945 (*via Suzi Holenchak Riddle*)

Right
In one of the war's odd coincidences, the P-40L that 1Lt George R 'Bob' Bolte flew in the 85th FS/79th FG returned to the United States before he did! Bolte, left, with fellow ex-'Flying Skull' pilots Bill Mathesius and John Hoagland, found *"Stinkeroo"* at Newark Airport awaiting scrapping when he got home to New Jersey in 1944. Bolte shot down one Bf 109 and damaged two Fw 190s during his combat tour (*Bob Bolte*)

Clusters of fragmentation bombs were a common load slung beneath the wings or central fuselage of 324th FG P-40s during 1944, as the group hounded German lines of communication in Italy (*Bruce Hunt*)

then the Warhawk pilots encountered a mixed formation of Fw 190s and Bf 109s south-east of Rome.

Fenex quickly shot down one Fw 190, then chased another one north-west for three miles before bringing it down as well. He also damaged two more Fw 190s, while 2Lt James Dealy shot down an Fw 190 and 1Lt William R King damaged a Bf 109. Fenex's two victories brought his total to five, making him the last P-40 ace in the MTO.

The situation at Anzio stabilised, but the invasion forces there were unable to advance on Rome, and the main Allied army remained bottled up to the south by the German forces holding the high ground at Cassino. On 12 May, the 5th Army specifically requested the 324th FG, known for the accuracy of its bombing, to attack German positions on Monastery Hill with phosphorus and fragmentation anti-personnel bomb clusters.

Fighting their way through bad weather and heavy ground fire, 24 P-40 pilots dropped more than five tons of bombs with pinpoint accuracy, effectively eliminating German resistance without harming friendly troops just 300 yards away. Then 12 more Warhawks came in to dive-bomb and strafe enemy troops massing for a counterattack in a narrow gully on the hill. Again, the enemy threat went up in clouds of smoke and rubble, and at last Allied troops were able to clear the barrier at Monte Cassino.

Over a 26-day period the 324th FG had flown more than 100 missions per day in support of the advance on Rome, losing 21 P-40s in the process, but earning a second Distinguished Unit Citation.

On 13 May, P-40s tangled with German fighters for the last time. Again, Lts Dealy and King of the 316th FS were involved, each shooting down a Bf 109, as did 1Lt Ken Scheiwe of the 315th FS. Dealy and Lt Arthur Kusch were shot down, but Dealy was befriended by partisans who helped him evade capture and return to his squadron.

The 324th FG moved to the Anzio beachhead on 6 June 1944 and one week later moved again, this time to an airfield north of Rome. It was from this field, Monalto di Castro, that the 324th FG flew its last P-40 missions on 18 July 1944. Immediately thereafter, the pilots ferried their war-weary aeroplanes to Naples and traded them in for new P-47Ds. The Warhawk's long and bloody war in the Mediterranean Theater of Operations was over.

1Lt Kenneth D Scheiwe of the 315th FS/324th FG was involved in the Warhawk's last air battle in the MTO war. On 13 May 1944, he shot down one of three Bf 109s destroyed north of Rome by 324th FG pilots, who in turn lost two of their own. Scheiwe's P-40, named *MISS GINNA III* for the girlfriend who would later become his wife, carries a cluster of fragmentation bombs under its belly and six 40-pounders under its wings. The red diamond on the cowling is the 315th FS insignia (*McCracken photo via James V Crow*)

APPENDICES

Victories by Units* Operating the P-40 in the Ninth and Twelfth Air Forces

33rd FG

Headquarters – November 1942-February 1944 - 11 kills

58th FS – November 1942-February 1944 - 50 kills

59th FS – November 1942-February 1944 - 41 kills

60th FS – November 1942-February 1944 - 35 kills

99th FS** – June 1943-June 1944 (attached) - 17 kills

57th FG

Headquarters – October 1942-January 1944 - 1 kill

64th FS – August 1942-January 1944 - 42.5 kills

65th FS – August 1942-January 1944 - 40 kills

66th FS – August 1942-January 1944 - 60.5 kills

79th FG

Headquarters – November 1942-March 1944 - 1 kill

85th FS – December 1942-March 1944 - 31 kills

86th FS – December 1942-March 1944 - 18 kills

87th FS – December 1942-March 1944 - 42 kills

324th FG

Headquarters – March 1943-July 1944 - 2 kills

314th FS – March 1943-July 1944 - 37 kills

315th FS – May 1943-July 1944 - 6 kills

316th FS – March 1943-July 1944 - 21 kills

325th FG

Headquarters – April 1943-October 1943 - 12 kills

317th FS – May 1943-October 1943 - 52 kills

318th FS – April 1943-October 1943 - 36 kills

319th FS – April 1943-October 1943 - 36 kills

Total USAAF P-40 Victories in the MTO – 592

Notes

* - the 27th and 86th FGs also flew P-40s briefly during the spring of 1944, but scored no victories with the Warhawks

** - the 99th FS was also attached to the 79th, 324th and 86th FGs at various times before converting to P-47s in June 1944

Aces who flew P-40s with the Ninth and Twelfth Air Forces

Name	Unit	P-40 Victories	Notes
Maj Levi R Chase	60th FS/33rd FG	10	(also 2 kills in P-51 CBI)
Col William W Momyer	33rd FG HQ	8	
Capt Roy E Whittaker	65th FS/57th FG	7	
Capt Ralph G Taylor Jr	317th FS/325th FG	6	
Maj Robert L Baseler	325th FG HQ	5	(also 1 kill in P-47)
Maj John L Bradley	58th FS/33rd FG	5	
1Lt Robert J Byrne	64th FS/57th FG	5	
2Lt Arthur B Cleaveland	64th FS/57th FG	5	(all on 18 April 1943)
Capt Frank J Collins	319th FS/325th FG	5	
2Lt Richard E Duffy	314th FS/324th FG	5	(all on 18 April 1943)
Capt James E Fenex Jr	316th FS/324th FG	5	
1Lt Paul G McArthur	87th FS/79th FG	5	
Capt Lyman Middleditch Jr	64th FS/57th FG	5	
1Lt Robert J Overcash	64th FS/57th FG	5	
2Lt MacArthur Powers	314th FS/324th FG	5	(5 on 18 April 1943, and 2.25 kills in Spitfire with RAF)
1Lt Walter B Walker Jr	317th FS/325th FG	5	
Maj Mark E Hubbard	59th FS/33rd FG	4	(also 2.5 kills in P-51 ETO)
2Lt Alfred C Froning	65th FS/57th FG	3	(also 3 kills in P-47)
Capt Herschel H Green	317th FS/325th FG	3	(also 15 kills in P-47 & P-51)
2Lt George P Novotny	317th FS/325th FG	3	(also 5 kills in P-47)
2Lt Roy B Hogg	318th FS/325th FG	2	(also 4 kills in P-47 & P-51)
Flt Off Cecil O Dean	317th FS/325th FG	1	(also 5 kills in P-47 & P-51)
2Lt Richard W Dunkin	317th FS/325th FG	1	(also 8 kills in P-47 & P-51)

Note – Some sources also incorrectly list both 1Lt Wyman D Anderson (three kills and one damaged) of the 87th FS/79th FG and Capt Thomas T Williams of the 66th FS/57th FG as aces

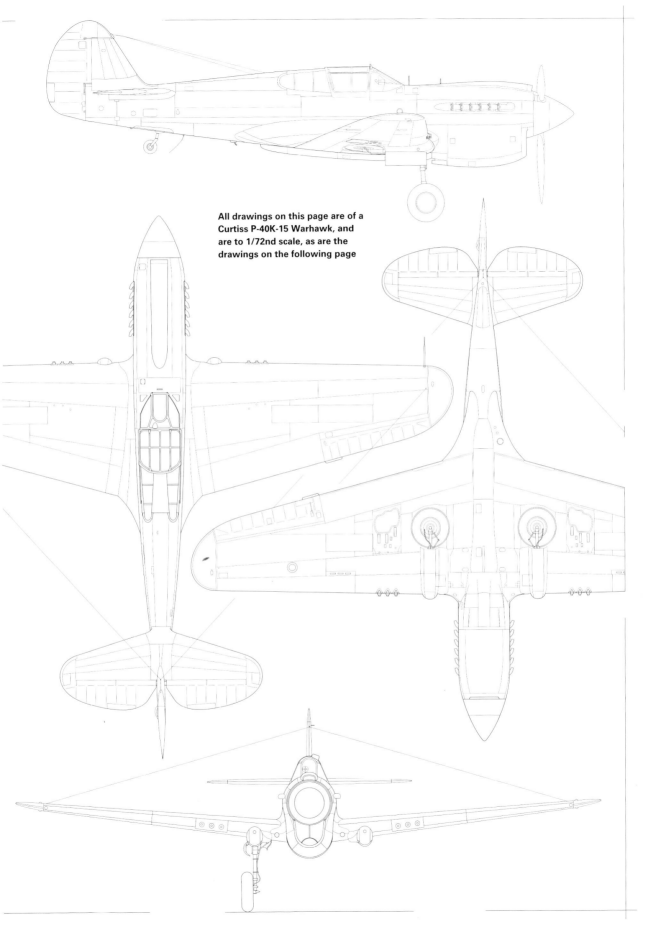

All drawings on this page are of a
Curtiss P-40K-15 Warhawk, and
are to 1/72nd scale, as are the
drawings on the following page

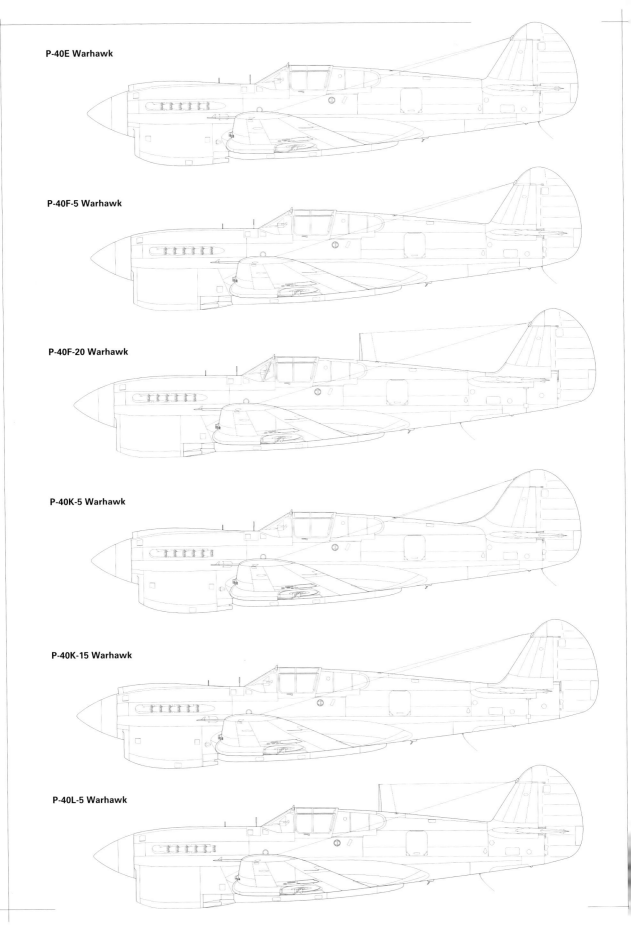

P-40E Warhawk

P-40F-5 Warhawk

P-40F-20 Warhawk

P-40K-5 Warhawk

P-40K-15 Warhawk

P-40L-5 Warhawk

1

P-40F-5 41-14315 of 2Lt James E Reed, 59th FS/33rd FG, Operation *Torch*, Port Lyautey, Morocco, 11 November 1942

Reed picked up this factory-fresh aeroplane at Harrisburg on 29 September 1942 and delivered it to Philadelphia. On 21 October 1942, he flew it to Norfolk, Virginia, where pilot and aeroplane were loaded aboard the aircraft carrier USS *Chenango* with 76 other P-40s of the 33rd FG. While en route to North Africa, Reed passed the time by cleaning his aeroplane's six 0.50-calibre machine guns, and painting his girlfriend's nickname, *RENEE*, on the engine cowling. The American flag invasion markings also were added whilst at sea. He launched off the carrier for Port Lyautey, French Morocco, on the fourth day of the Operation *Torch* invasion, 11 November 1942. Reed flew missions from Casablanca in this aeroplane for a month, before the P-40 was turned over to the Free French on 20 December 1942.

2

P-40F-20 41-19944 of Capt John L Bradley, 59th FS/33rd FG, Thelepte, Tunisia, 1 February 1943

Bradley, assigned to the 33rd Pursuit Group directly out of flying school in May 1941, was one of the senior pilots in the unit when it commenced combat operations in North Africa. It is believed he was flying this P-40F, recently transferred in from the 325th FG, on the morning of 1 February 1943 when he shot down two Ju 87s for his first kills. Bradley's aeroplane was hit during the fierce dogfight, and he was forced to bail out when its engine quit. He landed safely ten miles south of Maknassy, and had returned to his base at Thelepte by the end of the day. Soon thereafter Bradley transferred to the 58th FS as its commanding officer, and he went on to score three more times to become the unit's only ace.

3

P-40L-5 42-10600 of Maj Levi Chase, CO of the 60th FS/33rd FG, Sbeitla, Tunisia, April 1943

Chase was the only P-40 double ace in the MTO, scoring ten confirmed victories between 18 December 1942 and 5 April 1943. After achieving two kills twice with the 58th FS, he was appointed commanding officer of the 60th FS in January 1943. Chase picked up this replacement aircraft at the end of a two-week leave in Casablanca on 27 February 1943. Rejoining his unit at Berteaux, in Algeria, on 2 March, he scored the first of six victories in this aeroplane two weeks later. As far as is known, Chase's P-40L carried no unit or personal markings, save the test victory tallies (nine swastikas and one fasces) below the cockpit. He scored two further victories in 1945, flying a P-51D with the 2nd Air Commando Group in Burma, and he returned to combat in Korea as commander of the F-80-equipped 8th Fighter-Bomber Wing.

4

P-40L-20 42-11094 of Maj Charles H Duncan, CO of the 59th FS/33rd FG, Licata, Sicily, August 1943

Duncan, one of the original Operation *Torch* pilots, scored four victories as operations officer of the 58th FS prior to assuming command of the 59th FS from 4 May 1943. The name on the aeroplane honoured Duncan's wife, Jane. During flight training, Duncan had picked up the nickname 'Dugan', which was soon shortened to 'Duge'. After he got married in January 1942, Duncan's friends began calling his wife 'Little Duge'. Four Bf 109 silhouettes behind the name symbolise his confirmed victories, and the white tail stripe was a unit marking adopted by the 59th FS in the summer of 1943. The main and tail wheel hubcaps were white with a red stripe.

5

P-40L-5 42-10568 of Col William W Momyer, CO of the 33rd FG, Paestum, Italy, Autumn 1943

As commanding officer, Momyer led the 33rd FG off the USS *Chenango* to Port Lyautey on 10 November 1942. Between then and October 1943 he scored eight confirmed victories, including four Ju 87s on 31 March 1943. This, his last P-40 in the 33rd FG, borrowed its name – *SPIKE* – and nose art from Momyer's own nickname. It also displayed the yellow tail stripe of the 60th FS, yellow wing bands and red-white-blue hubcaps divided into 'pie slices'. The location of Momyer's eight victory markers mid-fuselage was highly unusual. A career USAF officer, Momyer rose to command Tactical Air Command as a four-star general before retiring in 1973.

6

P-40L-5 42-10536 of Lt Ralph L Griffith, 58th FS/33rd FG, Naples, Italy, January 1944

Two pilots named Ralph L Griffith flew in the 58th FS. Typical unsung fighter-bomber pilots, both men earned air medals in recognition of their combat records, but neither had an opportunity to file claims for enemy aircraft destroyed in the air. One of the Griffiths flew this P-40L toward the end of the 33rd FG's tour in the MTO. It featured the red tail stripe of the 58th FS, a winged Petty girl nose art and the name *Gerry* on the engine cowling, plus a white ring around the hubcaps of the main landing gear.

7

P-40F-1 (serial unknown) 'White 01' of Col Frank H Mears, CO of the 57th FG, Muqueibila, Palestine, August 1942

Mears, commander of the 57th FG, flew this aircraft off the USS *Ranger* to Accra, on the African Coast, on 19 July 1942 to lead the first-ever deployment of a complete USAAF fighter group into a combat zone from an aircraft carrier. On first arriving in the combat theatre, the P-40Fs of the 57th FG displayed only aeroplane-in-group numbers and occasional personal markings. The desert sand camouflage was sprayed over the aeroplanes' factory-applied Olive Drab top colour prior to their delivery to the group. The red diamonds on the nose were a carryover marking from the 57th's pre-war days. Mears, one of the original officers assigned to the group when it formed in 1941, led the 57th until December 1942, when he was posted to Ninth Air Force Fighter Command.

8

P-40K-1 42-46046 'White 13' of 1Lt R Johnson 'Jay' Overcash, 64th FS/57th FG, Hani Main, Tunisia, May 1943

Overcash started his combat tour as a member of the 66th FS, but scored four of his five aerial victories after transferring to the 64th FS in November 1942. This P-40K-1 was assigned to the 64th as a replacement aircraft when its supply of P-40Fs began to dwindle during the advance into Tunisia. It bears the squadron's 'Black Scorpions' badge on the nose and Overcash's personal skull marking below the cockpit, in addition to five swastikas denoting his tally of victories. This profile's fuselage number has been determined by a study of 64th FS combat reports. Overcash scored his final two victories in this aircraft on the afternoon of 26 April 1943.

9

P-40F-10 41-14596 'White 10' of Capt Arthur E Exon, CO of the 64th FS/57th FG, Scordia, Sicily, August 1943

Exon was one of the early replacement pilots to join the 64th FS, and he went on to assume command of the squadron in July 1943. He shot down a Bf 109 for his first aerial victory during the famous 'Palm Sunday Massacre' mission of 18 April 1943, then scored again nearly a year later flying a P-47. Following 64th FS tradition, Exon flew aircraft 'White 10' as the squadron commander. This fighter later served as a hack with the 461st BG in Italy. Exon completed 135 combat missions for a total of 325 combat hours. His tour came to a premature end during a mission over Cecina, in Italy, in April 1944, when an exploding ammunition depot damaged his P-47 and he was forced to bail out. Captured by the Germans, Exon remained a prisoner of war until June 1945.

10

P-40F-1 41-13947 'White 46' of 1Lt Gilbert O Wymond Jr, 65th FS/57th FG, LG 174, Egypt, October 1942

Gil Wymond probably served longer in the 65th FS than any other pilot during the war. One of those who flew off the USS *Ranger*, he was named squadron commander in May 1943, and held the job for two years while flying 140 combat missions and scoring three aerial victories. This P-40 was his first of 16 assigned aircraft to carry the name *HUN HUNTER*. Oddly, it wears two swastika kill markers, although Wymond's first two victories were over Italian CR.42 biplanes on 27 October 1942. He featured prominently in the wartime documentary film *Thunderbolt*, which told the story of 65th FS operations over Italy in 1944 during Operation *Strangle*.

11

P-40F-1 41-14081 'White 43' of Capt Roy E 'Deke' Whittaker, 65th FS/57th FG, Hani Main, Tunisia, April-May 1943

Whittaker, top ace of the 57th FG, flew two similarly-marked Warhawks during his combat tour, and this was the second of them. The first was transferred to the 66th FS in December 1942 and renumbered 'White 96'. This aeroplane carries Whittaker's full score of seven victories, and it also displays the 65th FS 'Fighting Cocks' badge on the nose. As with Wymond's aeroplane, swastikas were used for all kill markers, although two of Whittaker's victims were Italian aircraft. His most successful combat mission was 18 April 1943, when he shot down three Ju 52/3m transports and a Bf 109 during the 'Palm Sunday Massacre'. *Miss Fury* was lost in October 1943, several months after Whittaker had completed his combat tour.

12

P-40F (serial unknown) 'White 47' of 1Lt Alfred C Froning, 65th FS/57th FG, Amendola, Italy, November 1943

As the 57th FG's last ace, Froning scored the first three of his six victories on P-40s, although none in this aircraft, which had the inscription *HOT LIPS* painted on its wings above the gun barrels. Joining the 65th FS as a replacement in January 1943, Froning was shot down by ground fire on his 11th mission, but landed safely and was able to rejoin his unit. He shot down two Ju 52/3ms on the Palm Sunday mission, and scored again on 30 April 1943 over the Gulf of Tunis. After a six-month dry spell, Froning downed two Bf 109s on 16 December 1943 during one of the 57th FG's first P-47 missions, and went on to claim his last victory a month later. He completed 117 missions with the 65th FS.

13

P-40F-1 (serial unknown) 'White 84' of 2Lt Dale R Deniston, 66th FS/57th FG, LG 91, Egypt, October 1942

Deniston was assigned this aircraft at Mitchell Field, New York, in June 1942, and he flew it off the USS *Ranger* when the 57th FG deployed to Africa the following month. Deniston completed 100 missions during his tour of duty with the 66th FS, but he never had the opportunity to register an aerial victory. This aeroplane, however, was the one in which Jay Overcash scored his first kill on 26 October 1942. It was later emblazoned with the 66th FS's 'Exterminators' badge on the nose, and had the name *Robin* repeated in large letters on the upper engine cowling.

14

P-40F-1 41-13970 'White 95' of 2Lt William B Williams, 66th FS/57th FG, Gambut, Libya, November 1942

Williams was shot down by Bf 109s in this aircraft on 11 January 1943 while flying top cover for an armed reconnaissance mission – no trace of Williams or *Count Pistof* was ever found. As shown here, the aeroplane displays typical 57th FG operational markings for late 1942. Not visible are the large, white stars on its hubcaps or the non-standard fin flash on the right side of the tail, which displayed the colours red-white-blue left to right, not front to back.

15

P-40K-1 (serial unknown) 'White 71' of Capt George W 'Pop' Long, 66th FS/57th FG, Cape Bon, Tunisia, May 1943

The 66th FS received its first P-40K-1 replacement aircraft in December 1942, and this one was assigned to Long, who commanded A Flight. The two-tone upper camouflage is unusual for 57th FG P-40Ks, most of which were painted overall desert tan. The aeroplane also had white rings painted on its hubcaps. The nickname *POP* referred to the fact that Long's wife had been pregnant when he was ordered overseas, and she delivered their first child while he was serving in North Africa. Long destroyed two Ju 52/3ms and damaged a Bf 110 on the Palm Sunday mission.

16

P-40F-1 (serial unknown) 'White X01' of Lt Col Earl Bates, CO of the 79th FG, Causeway LG, Tunisia, March 1943

To Bates fell the difficult job of assuming command of the

79th FG in November 1942 after his popular predecessor, Lt Col Peter McGoldrick, was killed in action on his first combat mission. This P-40 was the first of three named *Lil Joe* (and featuring the 79th FG crest on the nose) that Bates flew in combat. The group used the 'X' prefix on its aeroplane-in-group numbers to differentiate its Warhawks from those of the other Ninth Air Force fighter units. Although he did an outstanding job as group commander, Bates scored no aerial victories before leaving the group in May 1944 to assume command of the 86th FG.

17
P-40F-5 (serial unknown) 'White X21' of Capt Samuel L Say, 85th FS/79th FG, Hani West, Tunisia, May 1943
Attached to the 64th FS/57th FG for combat experience when he first arrived in the combat zone, Say registered the first aerial claim by a 79th FG pilot when he damaged a Bf 109 on 8 December 1942 near the Egypt-Libya border. He went on to destroy Bf 109s on 30 April and 8 May 1943 while flying with his own squadron. Although this was his regularly assigned P-40, he scored neither of his victories in it. The aeroplane wears the 85th's 'Skeeters' badge on its cowling. Say was very appreciative of his crew chief, S/Sgt Ken Comeaux. 'This aeroplane did everything it was supposed to and never missed a beat', he told the author years later. 'Comeaux was like a mother hen, and he maintained the smoothest engine ever flown'.

18
P-40F-20 (serial unknown) 'White X17' of 1Lt Robert J Duffield, 85th FS/79th FG, Capodichino, Italy, February 1944
Duffield's successes against enemy aircraft came late in his combat tour, when he scored victories in this well-worn Warhawk on 25 January and 7 February 1944. Note how the fighter's serial number has been painted out on the rudder, and the half-hearted effort made to add bars to the fuselage national insignia without disrupting the aeroplane-in-squadron number. The name *Lee's Hope* was left over from a previous operator, and Duffield later changed it to *Speedy Edie*. As he told the author, 'She died on her 91st mission'.

19
P-40F-15 41-19735 'White X48' of 1Lt Wayne E Rhynard, 86th FS/79th FG, Hani West, Tunisia, May 1943
The P-40F-15 was supposed to be a cold-weather version of the Merlin-powered Warhawk, but that did not stop them from finding their way to North Africa, as did Rhynard's *Lucifer's Ghost*. Rhynard served as D Flight commander in the 86th FS, completing 84 missions between March and September 1943. He shot down one Bf 109 and damaged a second during a swirling dogfight near Tunis on 30 April 1943. Rhynard returned to combat in 1944-45 with the Eighth Air Force in England.

20
P-40F-20 41-19936 'White X83' of 1Lt Paul G McArthur, 87th FS/79th FG, Hani West, Tunisia, June 1943
McArthur has the distinction of being the 79th FG's only ace. On 10 June 1943 he shot down four of the 14 enemy fighters claimed by the 87th FS in a wild dogfight over Pantellaria

Island, then bailed out of 'White X83' over the sea – a British destroyer rescued him the following day. McArthur's last victory came on 13 August 1943, when he shot down a Bf 109 during a dive-bombing mission over Sicily. No photographic record of 'White X83' is known to exist, but its serial number was determined by cross-checking P-40 airframe history records. An Alabama native, McArthur returned to combat during the Korean War as a B-29 pilot, and then became a lawyer after retiring from the USAF in 1966.

21
P-40F-15 41-19746 'White X81' of 1Lt Charles 'Jazz' Jaslow, 87th FS/79th FG, Causeway LG, Tunisia, March 1943
Jaslow scored his lone confirmed victory in 'White X81' on 2 April 1943 during an escort mission over the Akarit line. Bounced from above by a flight of Bf 109s, Jaslow turned into his attackers and opened fire, then watched as one of the Bf 109s continued diving straight into the sea. Jaslow completed 80 missions with the 87th FS and returned home to the US in November 1943. His fighter had a checkerboard pattern painted on its hubcaps in yellow and black.

22
P-40L-15 42-10855 'White A33' of 1Lt Robert W Deiz, 99th FS/79th FG, Capodichino, Italy, 27 January 1944
The all-black 99th FS identified its P-40s with the prefix 'A' ahead of the aeroplane-in-squadron number. Deiz, an early Tuskegee Airman, was flying 'White A33' on the morning of 27 January 1944 over the beachhead at Anzio when his formation was attacked by Fw 190s. He scored one of the five confirmed victories awarded to 99th FS pilots for the mission, the unit's first major success in air-to-air combat after eight months of operations. Deiz scored again the following day in another P-40L. After returning to the US, Deiz volunteered to return to combat in the B-25-equipped 477th BG, but the unit was still at Tuskegee when the war ended.

23
P-40F-1 41-14282 'White Y20' of 2Lt MacArthur Powers, 314th FS/324th FG, El Kabrit, Egypt, February 1943
Powers, a New Yorker, joined the RAF in 1941 and scored 2.25 victories flying Spitfire VBs with No 145 Sqn in North Africa. He transferred to the USAAF in January 1943, and was made B Flight leader within the 314th FS in order to make the most of his combat experience. Powers encountered enemy aircraft only once more, but that was all he needed to become an ace. He was leading the 314th FS in this aircraft on 18 April 1943 – the famous Palm Sunday mission – when he shot down four Ju 52/3m transports and a Bf 109 over the Gulf of Tunis. He remained in the USAF after the war and retired as a lieutenant colonel in 1963.

24
P-40F-1 (serial unknown) 'White Y10' of Maj Robert F Worley, CO of the 314th FS/324th FG, El Kabrit, Egypt, February 1943
The original commanding officer of the 314th FS, Worley flew this aircraft until he was shot down by a Bf 109 over Cape Bon on his squadron's first mission, on 13 March 1943. Wounded, he belly-landed 'White Y10' in enemy territory and

succeeded in making his way back to Allied territory on foot. A superior pilot, and well respected by his men, Worley continued to lead the 314th until he completed his combat tour in February 1944. He flew 120 combat missions with the unit, but made no claims for aerial victories. Worley made a career in the USAF and rose to the rank of major general, but he was shot down and killed flying an RF-4C Phantom over South Vietnam on 23 July 1968.

25
P-40L-1 42-10436 'White 11' of Capt Bruce E Hunt, 314th FS/324th FG, Cercola, Italy, November 1943

This Warhawk started life in the 325th FG as the mount of ace Capt Ralph Taylor. It then went to the 314th FS when the 'Checkertails' transitioned to P-47s, and was assigned to Hunt, hence the fresh Olive Drab paint on the tail surfaces and mid-fuselage covering its previous markings. The name and Petty girl on the nose were carried over from its time with Capt Taylor. Hunt joined the 314th FS fresh out of flight school in July 1942 and moved up through the ranks as assistant operations officer, C Flight commander, operations officer and finally squadron commander. In 172 combat missions he destroyed one Bf 109, plus one probably destroyed and one damaged.

26
P-40L-5 42-10653 'White 01' of Col William K 'Sandy' McNown, CO of the 324th FG, Cercola, Italy, December 1943

McNown transferred from the 33rd FG to form the new 324th FG in July 1942, and he built it from a paper organisation into one of the top fighter-bomber groups in the MTO. He flew this distinctively-marked Warhawk late in his combat tour, before relinquishing command of the 324th FG on Christmas Day 1943 to become executive officer of the 64th FW. Note the distinctive 324th FG crest on the nose. A participant in the Palm Sunday 1943 mission, McNown elected to fly in a wingman position that day and received credit for shooting down two Ju 52/3ms.

27
P-40F-15 41-19740 'White Y10' of 1Lt Richard T Conly, 315th FS/324th FG, Kairouan, Tunisia, May 1943

Conly, 315th FS operations officer, only had about a week of combat experience when he shot down a C.202 for his squadron's first aerial victory, and probably destroyed a second one, on 29 April 1943. His unit's mission on this day was to provide top cover for a flight of P-40s from the 86th FS/79th FG that was dive-bombing in the Cape Bon area. This aircraft, named for Conly's wife, had yellow hubcaps with beer steins painted on them. Conly registered one more claim, for a Bf 109 damaged, on 25 January 1944.

28
P-40F-20 41-19988 'White 42' of 1Lt James Kirkendall, 315th FS/324th FG, Cercola, Italy, Autumn 1943

Although he scored no aerial victories, Kirkendall was one of the most highly regarded pilots in the 315th FS. He was serving as the unit's commander in July 1944 when he led the squadron's last P-40 combat mission – this aeroplane featured a white ring on its hubcaps. A career officer,

Kirkendall was given command of the 40th FS/35th FG, at Yokota Air Base, Japan, in March 1949. When the Korean War started, his squadron was one of the first ordered into combat. While in Korea, from 1950 to 1951, Kirkendall flew 104 combat missions. He retired from the USAF as a major general.

29
P-40F-20 (serial unknown) 'White 49' of 1Lt David L Giltner, 315th FS/324th FG, Pignataro, Italy, Spring 1944

Giltner, a replacement pilot who joined the 315th FS in April 1944, flew this much-travelled Warhawk before his squadron converted to P-47s. The aeroplane began its operational career in the 64th FS/57th FG as 1Lt Bruce Abercrombie's *Ginger*, which explains the name on the upper cowling. Next, the Warhawk went to the 315th FS, where it picked up the red diamond marking on the lower cowling. 'White 49' was initially assigned to Capt Art Marks, the squadron's operations officer, who called it *Christel*. When Marks completed his combat missions, the fighter was passed on to Giltner. He renamed it *Marge* on the left side and *Judy* on the right, after his wife and daughter. It also had white-ringed hubcaps.

30
P-40F-15 41-19736 'White Y76' of Lt W S 'Buck' Buchanan Jr, 316th FS/324th FG, Cape Bon, Tunisia, June 1943

Buchanan was one of the original pilots in the 316th FS, known as the 'Hell's Belles'. He flew this Warhawk from the beginning of his tour until 8 July 1943, when it was severely damaged by a C.202 during an air battle over Sicily. Buchanan nursed 'White Y76' back to his base at Cape Bon with its engine barely running and a huge hole in the upper fuselage behind the cockpit. The rudder cable snapped when he touched down, so Buchanan had to steer the aeroplane with its brakes to get it back to the line. He was unhurt, but the Warhawk never flew again. Buchanan went on to fly 101 missions before returning home in February 1944.

31
P-40L-5 42-10664 'White 70' of Maj Paul T O'Pizzi Jr, CO of the 316th FS/324th FG, Cercola, Italy, Spring 1944

O'Pizzi first saw action with the 314th FS, scoring two victories over Sicily in July 1943. He transferred to the 316th FS several months later, and assumed command of his new squadron in January 1944. O'Pizzi scored his third victory on 16 February 1944 when he shot down an Fw 190 over the Anzio beachhead while flying this aircraft. Another hand-me-down from the 325th FG, this Warhawk had originally been assigned to group CO Lt Col Gordon Austin, who called the aeroplane *Lighthouse Louie*. Note how its former fuselage number 'White 44' and checkertail markings have been painted out. The hubcaps on its main landing gear were red.

32
P-40F-20 41-20006 of Lt Col Robert Baseler, CO of the 325th FG, Mateur, Tunisia, September 1943

Baseler scored his first five victories in this specially-modified Warhawk before it was repainted in this striking scheme and taken off operations. The two outboard guns were removed, along with the radio and other non-essential items, to lighten the aeroplane in the hope of making it capable of reaching high-altitude German photo-reconnaissance aircraft. Although its performance was much improved, Baseler never did catch one of the high-flying raiders. The aeroplane originally carried the name *MORTIMER SNERD* on the right side upper engine cowling, but it is not known if the name survived the repainting. Baseler added one more victory while flying a P-47 to bring his total to six.

33

P-40L-5 42-10866 'White 59' of Capt John C A Watkins, 325th FG HQ, Mateur, Tunisia, September 1943

Watkins, the 325th FG operations officer, was a former staff officer for Gen H H Arnold, chief of the USAAF. He is credited with obtaining permission for the 325th FG to adopt its distinctive checkertail markings. Watkins scored three kills during the summer of 1943, including two Bf 109s over Sardinia on 28 August. The fuselage number 'White 59' of this, his third P-40, indicates it was maintained by the 318th FS. Watkins had the unusual circumstance of serving with his brother in the 325th FG. Sadly, Flt Off William Watkins was killed in December 1943 when he and two other pilots crashed their P-47s into an Italian mountain in bad weather.

34

P-40F-10 (serial unknown) 'White 28' of 1Lt Herschel H 'Herky' Green, 317th FS/325th FG, Mateur, Tunisia, August 1943

Green, top ace of the 325th FG, scored the first three of his eventual 18 kills while flying P-40s. This was his third Warhawk, and it is shown here as it appeared when first assigned to him. The fuselage number was soon changed to 'White 11', and it probably had the group's trademark black and yellow checkers applied to its tail surfaces as well. His initials *HHG* appear in the emblem on the nose. It's likely that Green scored a Bf 109 probably destroyed on 28 April 1943 while flying this P-40. He scored ten victories in P-47s and his final five in P-51s.

35

P-40L-1 42-10436 'White 13' of Capt Ralph G 'Zack' Taylor Jr, 317th FS/325th FG, Mateur, Tunisia, August 1943

Taylor, 317th FS operations officer, became the first ace of the 325th FG when he scored a triple victory – two C.202s and a Bf 109 destroyed – in this P-40 on 20 July 1943 near Decimomannu, Sicily. Some references suggest that P-40L-1s shared the short fuselage of the P-40F-1, but this aircraft provides evidence to the contrary. Taylor obtained the fighter in a trade with his friend 'Herky' Green after Green was shot up in sit on his first mission. As noted in profile 25, this P-40 later flew the 324th FG. Green made a career in the USAF, flying F-86s in Korea and retiring in 1971 as a major general.

36

P-40L-20 42-11050 'White 17' of Flt Off Cecil O Dean, 317th FS/325th FG, Mateur, Tunisia, May 1943

Dean spent 14 months as an enlisted aeroplane mechanic in the Army before being accepted into flight school in 1941. Assigned to the 317th FS in September 1942, he began his combat career in this Warhawk the following spring. He was flying this aeroplane on 30 July 1943 when he shot down a Bf 109 for his first victory. Three successes in P-47s and two

in P-51s followed. On 2 July 1944 he collided with his wingman near Budapest and was forced to bail out of his Mustang. He was captured and spent the rest of the war as a POW. Dean stayed in the USAF after the war, and spent time in Strategic Air Command before retiring in 1964.

37

P-40L-20 42-11098 'White 30' of Flt Off William T Tudor, 317th FS/325th FG, Mateur, Tunisia, June 1943

Tudor, like Cecil Dean, scored his first victory on the 30 July 1943 mission. In Tudor's case, however, it was his only confirmed victory of the war. During the mission – a sweep over southern Sardinia – the 317th FS was jumped at 9000 ft by a large group of Bf 109s and C.202s. The P-40s quickly gained the advantage, and when the scrap ended the 325th FG pilots claimed 21 victories for the cost of one P-40 shot down. Tudor's *LADY MACDEATH* was fitted with six wing guns, rather than the four found in most P-40Ls.

38

P-40F-15 41-19896 'White 25' of 1Lt Walter B 'Bud' Walker Jr, 317th FS/325th FG, Mateur, Tunisia, August 1943

Walker was the top scorer of the 30 July 1943 mission over Sardinia, being credited with three Bf 109s destroyed and also being slightly wounded during the fight. This brought his score to five confirmed, and made him the 325th FG's third ace. Ten days later, Walker was presented with a Purple Heart by Hollywood movie star Frances Langford when she and comedian Bob Hope visited the group with a USO troupe. Walker completed his combat tour of 50 missions shortly thereafter with no further opportunities to add to his score.

39

P-40L-5 42-10664 'White 40' of Capt Joseph D Bloomer, CO of the 318th FS/325th FG, Mateur, Tunisia, September 1943

Originally assigned to the 85th FS/79th FG out of flight school, Bloomer transferred to the 318th FS in September 1942. He scored four confirmed kills and rose to command of his squadron before completing his combat tour in the autumn of 1943. The colourful drop tank under the belly of *TRIXIE* is actually a home-made firebomb, which reportedly worked quite effectively. The P-40 also displayed 43 mission markers below the windscreen on its right side, and it was one of the first to carry the 318th 'Green Dragons' badge on its nose.

40

P-40L-1 42-10476 'White 89' of Flt Off John W Smallsreed, 319th FS/325th FG, Mateur, Tunisia, 20-26 May 1943

Smallsreed was one of the most promising pilots in the 319th FS during its early missions from North Africa. The Ohio native scored his first victory on 19 May 1943 over the Gulf of Cagliari, when the 325th FG claimed six Bf 109s destroyed for the loss of two P-40s. The next day, Smallsreed destroyed a huge Me 323 transport near Villacidro, and on 27 May 1943 he got his third victory – a Bf 109 shot down during an escort mission to Sardinia. Smallsreed failed to return from a mission flown 24 hours later. Bf 109s attacked the P-40s as they were escorting B-26s over Sicily, and no one saw what happened to the young pilot, who was listed as missing in action.

INDEX

References to illustrations are shown in **bold**. Plates are shown with page and caption locators in brackets.

FIND OUT MORE ABOUT OSPREY

❑ Please send me a FREE trial issue
of Osprey Military Journal

❑ Please send me the latest listing of Osprey's publications

❑ I would like to subscribe to Osprey's e-mail newsletter

Title/rank _____

Name _____

Address _____

_____

_____

Postcode/zip _____ state/country _____

e-mail _____

Which book did this card come from?

_____

❑ I am interested in military history

My preferred period of military history is _____

❑ I am interested in military aviation

My preferred period of military aviation is _____

I am interested in (please tick all that apply)

❑ general history   ❑ militaria   ❑ model making
❑ wargaming   ❑ re-enactment

Please send to:

USA & Canada: Osprey Direct USA, c/o Motorbooks
International, P.O. Box 1, 729 Prospect Avenue, Osceola,
WI 54020

UK, Europe and rest of world:
Osprey Direct UK, P.O. Box 140, Wellingborough, Northants,
NN8 2FA, United Kingdom

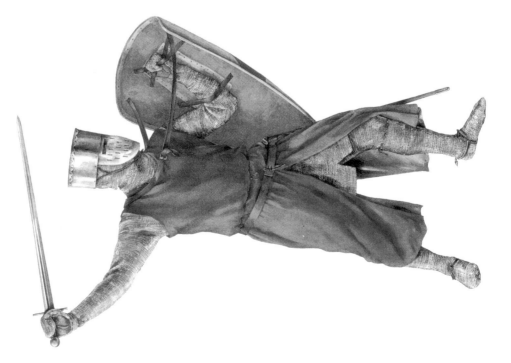

OSPREY
PUBLISHING

www.ospreypublishing.com

call our telephone hotline
for a free information pack

USA & Canada: 1-800-458-0454
UK, Europe and rest of world call:
+44 (0) 1933 443 863

Young Guardsman
Figure taken from *Warrior 22:*
Imperial Guardsman 1799–1815
Published by Osprey
Illustrated by Christa Hook

Knight, c.1190
Figure taken from *Warrior 1: Norman Knight 950 – 1204AD*
Published by Osprey
Illustrated by Christa Hook

POSTCARD